on track ...
Tears For Fears

every album, every song

Paul Clark

sonicbondpublishing.com

Sonicbond Publishing Limited
www.sonicbondpublishing.co.uk
Email: info@sonicbondpublishing.co.uk

First Published in the United Kingdom 2022
First Published in the United States 2022

British Library Cataloguing in Publication Data:
A Catalogue record for this book is available from the British Library

Typeset in ITC Garamond & ITC Avant Garde
Printed and bound in England

Graphic design and typesetting: Full Moon Media

on track ...
Tears For Fears

every album, every song

Paul Clark

sonicbondpublishing.com

Acknowledgements

I'd like to thank Stephen Lambe at Sonicbond Publishing for giving me the chance to indulge my passion for all things Tears For Fears. I have been a fan of the band ever since I heard 'Mad World' for the first time as a nine-year-old back in 1982. Who knew that holding my cassette player to the radio to record that song would lead to one day writing a book on the band?

A note to the band; I have bought enough versions of your records (in all formats) down the years to make up for that initial illegal home taping. It wasn't me that killed the music industry.

Thanks, Mum, as always, thanks for your support and help. I'll know that you have read the book when you can list one more Tears For Fears song other than that 'one'. To Dad, sadly not here to see this being published. Thanks to Kevin, Susan, Max, and Lottie. To Viv, for putting up with my nerdiness and converting to the Tears For Fears cause.

Thanks to Chris (H), Chris (R), and Graham. My thanks for putting up with numerous Tears For Fears entries on the playlists that we put together during our lockdown (and beyond) Zoom catch-ups.

Thanks to The We4Poets; David, Stanley, Michael, and Trish, for all their encouragement of my creative endeavours down the years.

To all the various Tears For Fears Facebook fan forums that I am a member of, that kept the hope alive that there would eventually be a new album. These passionate fanbases often supplied those nuggets of information that gave me those 'I didn't know that moments' when I was writing this book.

on track ...

Tears For Fears

Contents

Introduction

With the universally positive reception that the 2022 album *The Tipping Point* received, it could be argued that the band prematurely used everybody loves a happy ending as an album title. Given what the band went through, both personally and professionally, to get their latest album released, it feels like the story of Tears For Fears has achieved a positive finale. That said, fans hope that *The Tipping Point* is the start of a new chapter and not the end of the road.

The album *Everybody Loves a Happy Ending* which announced the reunion of Curt and Roland in 2004, was well-received by fans (it is still much loved on fan forums), but it seemed to attract minimal interest elsewhere. It has been heartening to see the way that the band have been received since the release of 'The Tipping Point' single back in 2021.

Since then, it seems like the band had finally found a label and management that knew what to do with their prized asset. Forums buzzed with band activity as they popped up in numerous places both in the UK and around the world. Geography is seemingly not too much of an issue in the post-pandemic Zoom era. Their PR team worked wonders in getting them on podcasts, websites, magazine covers, newspaper features, morning TV shows, radio, all platforms of social media – even doing the football predictions on the BBC Sport website in December 2021. Who would have predicted that the two Janov advocates back in the 1980s would be discussing the finer details of their team's fight for a top-four finish in the Premier League? (NB. It's Manchester United)

The fact that there was an album to celebrate is a testament to the resolve of the band, especially given the issues that they faced in the years between albums. It was also an epic display of faith from a fanbase that had been promised a new album many times down the years but without any sign of that prospect ever being realised.

With such a recognisable back catalogue, there was always an interest in the band during the years between albums. This often took the form of interesting covers/interpretations, samples, or their songs appearing on soundtracks. Lorde reinterpreted 'Everybody Wants to Rule the World' uniquely in 2013 for *The Hunger Games* soundtrack – the song was subsequently used by the band as their intro music on their *Rule the World Tour* in 2019. There is also the famous reimagining of 'Mad World' by Gary Jules and Michael Andrews for the movie *Donnie Darko*.

Though the band have been dormant, they have played the social media game; Curt is a notable presence on Twitter and has taken part with Tim Burgess on the Tears For Fears listening parties; Roland dabbled with Twitter when he was promoting his novel *Sex, Drugs & Opera: There's Life After Rock 'n' Roll* but soon took a hasty retreat. You can't blame him for having second thoughts about using that particular platform, although he was always a thoughtful and engaging presence when he was on there.

There have been accolades in the last few years. They received one for an Outstanding Song Collection at the 2021 Ivor Novello Awards. *Songs from the Big Chair* was the subject of *The Classic Album* documentary series in 2020. The recognition has shown that there is still an appreciation for the band's music. Given that they have been around for over 40 years now, there have been several anniversaries along the way to celebrate their landmark albums. In every interview promoting those retrospectives, there would be a question about new material and the responses always hinted at the potential of a new album.

That new album has brought about a collection of songs that might not be instantly identified as typical for a Tears For Fears record to some ears, but then what *is* a typically Tears For Fears record? In the early 80s, they went from being a minimalist shoegazing electro/acoustic outfit to embracing anthemic progressive classic rock/pop in the middle of the decade. After that, they disappeared and metamorphized into a psychedelic prog-pop-soul band, with a side helping of The Beatles thrown in for good measure.

Curt Smith said in an interview with the streaming service, *Tidal* before the release of *The Tipping Point* about where he sees the band fitting in today: 'I don't think we're tied to a decade, and we've never viewed ourselves as a heritage act, even though other people may have. To me, it means that you have nothing valid to say now'.

As was shown with the release of *The Tipping Point*, getting the songs written is not that easy, but it is just as difficult to agree on what the composition of the album should be. Curt told Paul Sinclair at *Super Deluxe Edition* before the release of *The Tipping Point* about what constitutes a Tears For Fears album: 'The only definition I've ever been able to come up with is that it's the stuff we agree on. The nature of a partnership is that a lot of the time you're making concessions to the other party; you're giving some leeway. And there's only so far you can be pushed. But you know, where we converge and agree on things, that's the sound of Tears For Fears.' Roland Orzabal's response was to joke, 'that's why it takes so long to release anything'.

They have been recognised by their peers as an influential band, from awards to name checks, covers and samples. Groups such as MGMT, The 1975, and Smashing Pumpkins have acknowledged the influence of Tears For Fears. The band even got a name check in the credits of Dave Grohl's *Storyteller* book, in which the author said: 'If it weren't for my sister's record collection (Neil Young, Bowie, Tears For Fears, Squeeze, etc), I may have followed a life of only death metal and corpse paint. She should be thanked for saving you all from that happening'.

The best description of the band comes from Zane Lowe, who, in an interview with *Apple Music* prior to the release of *The Tipping Point,* called them 'the weirdest successful band'. In print, that might not be seen as complementary, but you can get his point. They have always been an atypical pop band. Even though it can be seen that they have been an influence in some quarters, Roland Orzabal did say in 2015, when discussing the band's more progressive elements, 'It's hard to be influenced by Tears For Fears because there are so many iterations of the band'. That may be true, but the legacy of their impressive songbook is there for all to see.

As well as being great songwriters, they have become a great live act down the years. A new album brings the expectation of new performances. Roland Orzabal speaking to *Tidal.com's* Craig Rosen, about the band's live set: 'When we started playing live again in the early 2000s, we were starting to increase the muso side of what we were doing. We've got so much in our back pocket. We can play the '80s hits; then we bring out 'Bad Man's Song'. Now, you tell me that's a typical '80s song. Of course, it isn't. It sounds like Little Feat. When we go up against the pure nostalgia bands, we tend to kick their asses. That sounds a bit arrogant, but we aim high. We don't always get there, but we aim high'.

The band aimed high in the summer of 2022 and this is seen by the rave reviews for the initial US and UK dates on their *Tipping Point* World Tour. Sadly, that was until it was postponed due to a rib injury suffered by Curt Smith just before a gig at Lytham St Annes, in the UK, in July 2022.

Funny How Time Flies

The city of Bath, in southwest England, is where it all came together for Roland Orzabal, Curt Smith, and Tears For Fears.

Roland Jaime Orzabal de la Quintana was born in Portsmouth on August 22, 1961. Orzabal was originally given the name Raoul, but his mother, Margaret, changed it to Roland two weeks after he was born because it sounded more 'English'. Roland is of French, Spanish, and Argentinian lineage and it is claimed that his maternal grandfather helped eject the Argentinian dictator Peron (husband of Eva). There is a plaque on the Argentine Pampas for Jose de la Quintana.

His parents ran an entertainment agency supplying artists for working men's clubs. Among the acts would include ventriloquists and country and western singers. Orzabal's mother was a stripper and would also train them. His father, George, recorded and produced the musicians on their books. It was this immersion into the entertainment world that would inspire Roland's future career path: 'I grew up idolising one singer in particular, who was the antithesis of my father. Black belt at judo, big guy, sounded like Elvis. I thought, 'Yup, that's what I wanted to do'', Orzabal said in 2013 in an interview with Wyndham Wallace for *The Quietus*.

Orzabal moved to Bath,at the age of 11, with his mum (and two brothers, Carlos and Julian) when her relationship with Roland's father ended.

Orzabal endured something of a difficult upbringing. His father was bedridden for most of Roland's childhood and was confined to his home. Indeed, Roland was only three when his father suffered a nervous breakdown. He had undiagnosed PTSD from the second world war and could be violent towards Roland's mother. The singer would later reflect upon these events in the song 'Women in Chains'. He said to *the Quietus* in 2013:

Curt and I are both the middle of three boys, and in my situation, there was domestic violence. There are a lot of people who have difficult childhoods. My childhood was the same as my two brothers and they didn't go around moaning about it! We can all make a big deal that we were council estate kids. But that was the biggest thing that upset me, that my dad would be physically violent towards my Mum. And it got so bad that in the end, she left.

The retreat into songwriting from an early age would also offer solace from the difficult home life. Orzabal said to *Songwriting Magazine* in 2022:

I played the guitar from age nine and whenever there was a bad atmosphere, which was 24/7, I would go into my bedroom and strum the guitar and find some kind of 'company'. I suppose – that's what Paul Simon calls it... When you're playing the guitar, you have a circular relationship with yourself and you're self-soothing. That is a remarkable thing about playing the guitar and singing; it's incredible how much of a calming effect it has on you.

Curt Smith was born on June 24, 1961, and grew up in Bath, England. He was named after the actor Curt Jürgens. His childhood was as difficult as Roland's. His parents worked constantly and he experienced a similar level of neglect. Curt Smith was quite rebellious as a child and would often find himself in various scrapes. Indeed, the first time that the pair met, Curt could not come out because he had been grounded after getting into a fight. The pair met through an introduction from a bass player friend of Roland's called Paul, who had known Curt from his previous school, leading to Roland and Curt forming their first heavy metal band together at the age of 14. This was on the back of Roland hearing Smith sing 'They came to my flat one time and heard me singing along to a Blue Öyster Cult record ['Then Came the Last Days of May'], of all things, and Roland asked if I wanted to sing for their band.' Smith said to *The Quietus* in 2013.

He strived for some attention and it is claimed that he stole a violin (which he gave to Orzabal) from his school. Smith came from a working-class background and Orzabal was more middle class, but both of their formative years were on the council estates of Bath.

However, Orzabal was the more precocious of the duo and he had cut his teeth in several bands long before Graduate and Tears For Fears. He was also the more bookish until he had a moment of revelation. He said to *The Quietus* in 2013:

> I was one of those people in school who used to work hard and then when I was about 17, or 18, I had a mental Copernican inversion, so instead of just following what I was being told and doing well and getting 'A's, I just started questioning everything. We were reading a lot of existentialism, both in French and in English, so that kind of set me off.

Orzabal's talents as a guitarist marked him out as a notable figure even in his teenage years and this led to him forming several bands. He said as he recounted the time to The Quietus: 'Because I was more advanced on the guitar, at school I gave guitar lessons. The guys who were learning guitar, we'd form a band, and it would go on and on like that'.

It was these first steps that most teenagers who have a passion for music tend to follow and it's as far as the local youth club that they go. For Roland Orzabal, in particular, there were flirtations with folk and heavy metal before he alighted on the idea for his next steps as a musician.

Graduate – Acting My Age

Personnel:
Roland Orzabal: vocals, lead guitar
Curt Smith: bass guitar, vocals
John Baker: rhythm guitar, vocals
Steve Buck: keyboards, flute
Andy Marsden: drums
Record label: Precision
Recorded by Glen Tommey and Tony Hatch
UK Release Date: May 1980
Highest Chart Placings: Didn't Chart
Run Time: 36:27

The Tears For Fears story starts not with synthesisers or the pairing of Roland and Curt, but with a folk band called the Baker Brothers, featuring Roland and John Baker. Roland Orzabal had taught his good friend John to play the acoustic guitar and the pair performed in the local pubs and clubs of Bath. One of their regular gigs was on a Saturday afternoon at a hairdressing salon. Their early repertoire included the pair doing Simon and Garfunkel covers. The US duo's soundtrack album *The Graduate* inspired the name of their next venture.

Graduate's first manager Colin Wyatt introduced Orzabal and Baker to drummer Andy Marsden. He, in turn, recommended the keyboard player Steve Buck, who he had seen playing in a local nightspot. They had tried out several bass players without any success. Orzabal then asked his guitarist friend, Curt Smith, whether he could play the bass. His response was, 'I can learn', which he did. That conversation heralded the start (or to be precise, rekindled, as they had played in several less serious youth club bands before) of the partnership of Roland and Curt.

When the band looked for a record deal, they soon realised that their folk stylings were out of step with the current trends. They jumped on the bandwagon of the prevailing post-punk, new-wave, mod-revivalists that had been on the charts. Their inspirations were bands like The Merton Parkas, The Chords, The Secret Affair, Madness, and Elvis Costello. These influences informed the sound of Graduate. In a *Record Collector* interview in 2014, Roland Orzabal told Paul Lester that Graduate was 'a watered-down version of those acts. Costello was a hero, as were Madness and The Specials'.

The band signed a publishing deal with producer Tony Hatch (writer of the *Crossroads* theme, a popular UK soap of the time), who subsequently offered the group to Pye Records. Graduate recorded their debut ten-track album *Acting My Age* at Crescent Studios Bath in January 1980, although they were so young that they had to wait for Orzabal's 18th birthday before they could sign a record deal.

They had little success in the UK, although they did support Judie Tzuke on an extensive tour. It was during this period that their first single, 'Elvis Must Play Ska', entered the lower reaches of the charts.

A tour of Spain brought about some level of success for the band, with a top ten hit there and some TV appearances, which can be found on YouTube. The vigorous 'Nutty Boys' gyrations of Orzabal are a sight to behold. The relative success of 'Elvis Must Play Ska' also brought about radio attention back home in the UK, with BBC Radio 1 playlisting the song for six weeks. This also brought Roland Orzabal his first songwriting royalties in the shape of a cheque for £3,000 – a welcome sum after years of being unemployed.

Acting My Age was primarily written by Orzabal. It contains some of his first attempts at songwriting for a public audience. He had been writing songs since he was seven or nine (accounts differ) but was still developing his craft. Every writer has juvenilia that they would prefer the world not to see or hear, but via Graduate his are available for everyone. The songs may be fairly primitive and shallow compared to what followed and some of the tracks have not aged that well, but they still have some charm.

It was a gruelling tour of Germany in October and November of 1980 that did for the band. The age-old cliché of musical differences reared its head. Roland and Curt were against the excessive touring, while the rest of the band wanted to continue touring (and partying) as they saw this as a way of improving as a band. Somewhere in Holland, the duo realised that this was not what they had signed up for. The pair were, as Orzabal recollected in 2022 when talking to *The Creative Independent* website, 'on a different philosophical path to the rest of the guys in Graduate. We also were...how can I put it? A little bit sensitive'.

Orzabal was yet to cover the subject areas he was to explore with the first Tears For Fears album, the themes on The Graduate album being quite generic; the songwriter finding his voice. *Acting My Age* is not bad and it is an interesting insight into someone developing their craft. It was a steep learning curve to get to the next stage in his development as a songwriter and vocalist and he had not yet found his sound. Indeed, the full span of his vocal ability would not come to the fore until *Songs from the Big Chair*.

In an interview before the release of *The Tipping Point*, Curt dismissed most of what they wrote at the time. He told *Stereogum*: 'We were young and we were writing little cute pop songs. They didn't have that much depth back then because we were kids. We were probably thinking about one thing, as 16 or 17-year-old boys do — girls. Being in a band was one of the best ways to meet girls'.

During this period, several future Tears For Fears alumni intersected. One such band was Neon, formed in 1979 by Pete Byrne and Rob Fisher (later of hit UK pop outfit Climie Fisher). They recorded their first single, 'Making Waves' in October 1980, bringing in Orzabal and Smith as session musicians – although nothing Curt and Roland recorded with them was ever released.

John Baker and Steve Buck would later join The Korgis, the band that had a big UK hit with 'Everybody's Gotta Learn Some Time'. That band also featured members of Stackridge, including Andy Davis, who would later be a keyboard player in the Tears For Fears touring band.

There are still copies of the album in circulation, especially on Discogs and eBay. The band's back catalogue can also be found on the usual streaming services. In 1986, Precision Records cashed in on the success of *Songs from the Big Chair* by releasing an eight-track 10' EP. This record uses the same picture sleeve as the original *Acting My Age* LP, although the track order is a bit different, and two of the songs from the original LP – 'Bad Dreams' and 'Shut Up' – are not included in this release.

The album was subsequently released on CD. In 1991, the German label Sequel Records issued an eleven-track CD simply titled *Graduate* (Roland is mistakenly credited as Orzabel on the Castle Communications 1991 releases). This disc featured the tracklisting from the *Acting My Age* re-release, with two versions of 'Shut Up'. It features the previously unreleased song 'I See Through You'. A second collection came out in 2001 when Sanctuary Records issued a 19-track disc version of *Acting My Age*, plus the non-album single 'Ambition', 'I See Through You', and seven previously unreleased demo songs from a planned second album.

The standard front cover of the album is the band posing with instruments dressed in their matching mod attire against a white backdrop.

'Acting My Age' (Roland Orzabal)
The title track's influences can be heard quite clearly in this opener, true of quite a lot of the songs on the album. The title track is driven by an energetic Curt Smith bassline and sparse guitars, with a rhythmic bounce to it that is reflective of the band's influences. It has a decent hook to it too. Orzabal's vocal style has Elvis Costello's mannerisms to the fore. The song was released as a single, but only in Spain to capitalise on the band's extensive touring in that part of the world. It is worth noting for collectors that the Spanish seven-inch single is one of the band's rarest releases.

'Sick and Tired' (Curt Smith)
The guitar chord riff that rings throughout this Curt Smith song has that Andy Summers staccato style that he employed so well on the early The Police records. Again, the bass playing of Curt Smith comes to the fore. Throw in a Squeeze-style musical motif before and after the chorus and you have the perfect distillation of the sound of many new wave bands of the time. There are some prog-style keyboards thrown into the mix too. The song can also be found on the flip side of the 'Elvis Should Play Ska' on the Spanish seven-inch Single.

'Ever Met a Day' (Roland Orzabal)
The band's second UK single was released in May 1980 (Precision PAR104), and it's a track that still gets an occasional outing on the radio in the UK. It's the strongest song in the Graduate repertoire with another great Curt Smith bassline with bits of The Police in there too, especially in the middle eight, where it has a 'Walking on the Moon'-style break. The intro's flute motif alone should

have propelled this to the upper reaches of the charts. It's the kind of hook that Orzabal developed a talent for by the time he got to write songs like 'Head Over Heels' on *Songs from the Big Chair* while there are themes of alienation running through it – a precursor of songs to come. The track had a further outing when they flipped the single for a March 1981 (Precision PAR117) release, with 'Shut Up' as the single A-side and 'Ever Met a Day' on the reverse.

'Dancing Nights' (Roland Orzabal)
File this one under album filler. The chorus and the middle eight are catchy, but the verses are forgettable, while the rhythm and the vocals give the song a passing similarity to the 10CC hit 'Dreadlock Holiday'. It also sounds similar to a few of the other numbers on the album. There is a noticeable difference between the vinyl release and the versions that appear on the CD releases. There is a long fade with studio chatter, almost segueing into the next song, while the CD version has no chatter and there is a noticeable gap between the songs.

'Shut Up' (Roland Orzabal)
To someone of my vintage, this jaunty number sounds like a school's TV programme theme. There is an annoying harmonising vocal during the chorus (and at other points throughout) and a discordant piano riff that sounds like the same effect used on David Bowie's 'Ashes to Ashes' which was released in the same year. Again, there are slight differences in the mixes on the CD re-releases and the original vinyl version.

'Elvis Should Play Ska' (Roland Orzabal)
Highest chart places: UK: 106
Flip over the record and the B-side of *Acting My Age* opens with the band's biggest hit. It's a mission statement that defines their overall sound, although it had had minimal chart success, peaking just outside the top 100. The single (Precision Par100) was released in March 1980 (with 'Julie Julie' on the B-side). The 'Elvis' in question is not the one born in Tupelo, Mississippi, but the artist formally known as Declan McManus. The lyrics reference several song titles from Costello's early catalogue, using some of the signature sounds that would have been employed by The Attractions at the time. Graduate drummer Andy Marsden, quoted on the Tears For Fears fan site *Memoryfades.com*, explained where the inspiration for the title came from:

> Roland had heard an interview given by Elvis Costello where he said that all ska groups at that time were simply 'one-hit wonders' trying to cash in on the mod revival. Roland felt that his comments were sour grapes because a lot of the songs on the charts at that time were doing better than Elvis Costello's songs. Because of this, Roland wrote 'Elvis Should Play Ska'. In other words – stop moaning and write a ska song yourself. It was a mickey-take.

Because of the style of this song, the record company latched onto the modish sound and kitted out the band in the suits that they wear on the album cover. It's another one with a strong offbeat, typical of Graduate's sound, the song kicking off with a great guitar riff, followed by a keyboard part that gives over to a staccato guitar that drives the song along in an out-and-out musical tribute to Elvis Costello, both lyrically and stylistically. It's hard to listen to and not start wanting to dance.

'Watching Your World' (Roland Orzabal)
This is another song on which Roland, although singing well, it is trying to sound like those bands that he was inspired by. Because of that, it sounds quite affected at times. There's a discernible cockney accent to his vocal style, although it's a decent song with a spiky guitar line running throughout. The swirling keyboard riff lifts the song and gives it its melodic hook.

'Love That is Bad' (Roland Orzabal)
As well as the ever-present nod to all things Costello, this song opens with a catchy guitar riff and bassline that is evocative of The Attractions. The distinctive keyboard line that underpins the song has echoes of UK contemporaries Squeeze. You even can hear a bit of UK singer-songwriter Tom Robinson in the mix too, especially with the shouts of '2,3,4' just before the last chord is struck. It is one of the album's catchiest numbers with several hooks to keep the listener engaged and an extended middle-eight/guitar solo adding some variation. Lyrically the song is summed up pretty well with the title.

'Julie Julie' (Roland Orzabal)
This is the most laidback song on the album. It's another love song. Lyrically it may have not stood the test of time, having a distinctly American west coast feel. It does have 'album filler' or a 'B-side' vibe about it, which is probably why it was more at home on the reverse of the debut single.

'Bad Dreams' (Roland Orzabal)
The opening riff sounds a bit like US band REM during their IRS years. That returns midway through the song and acts as the hook and again, Orzabal does his best Elvis Costello impression. It's the album's closer and longest track with an almost calming, lullaby quality – its repetitive mantra being the title. It's a lovely, gentle closer to an album that clocks in just under 40 minutes. The track would also appear as the B-side of 'Ambition' (Precision PAR111).

Bonus Tracks
The original album *Acting My Age* (Precision PAR001) was released in May 1980 and contained ten tracks. A start had already been made on the follow-up album before Roland and Curt left the band and the second album was to

be called *Ambition* with a single with the same title preceding it. Even though a reconfigured line-up was assembled, they never released another album. he songs from the lost second album were not released at the time, only coming out when the debut album was reissued on CD for the first time in 2001.

'Ambition' (Roland Orzabal)
Highest chart places: UK: did not chart.
This A-side (Precision PAR111) was written for the band's intended follow-up album. It was a single release in October 1980. 'Bad Dreams' as the B-side. It is in keeping with the jaunty sound of their first album, suggesting the band was still following their previous mod influences closely for their next release. The song has an unfussy arrangement and is driven along by a keyboard riff. The vocals from Orzabal seem to be at their most affected, the chorus is sung as a harmony asking the question 'have you no ambition?'. There may even be a kazoo thrown into the mix during the musical break.

'I See Through You' (Curt Smith)
This was one written and sung by Curt Smith with a bassline that is straight from the Elvis Costello songbook. It's the hook that gets you into the song and the guitar riff throughout is quite pleasing. There is a la-la refrain in the middle eight before the catchy bassline returns at the end of the song. A close sonic relation to 'Elvis Must Play Ska', it feels like it could have been a potential single release if the band had stayed together. It would certainly have been a stand-out track on the second album.

'Premature Baby' (Roland Orzabal)
The influence of UK band XTC is all over this track, which might explain its vocal style, feeling like Orzabal is attempting his best Andy Partridge impression. It's hard to sum up what's so annoying about this song; it could be the affected vocals or perhaps the percussive elements that crop up throughout. Even though the song starts promisingl, it's one to skip.

'Christ Look Upon Us' (Roland Orzabal)
This is quite a laid-back number with religious overtones in both its sound palette and title. There is even a boys' choir thrown into the mix. It's the longest track that Graduate released, showing some development in the influences on the band. There's a saxophone solo towards the end of the song giving the track a lounge jazz vibe – the sax is an instrument that feature would heavily in future songs written by Orzabal. But overall, the song feels like it's meandering before the end.

'Oh U Boys' (Roland Orzabal)
The inspirations for the song are apparent in its opening line. The reference to 'meet you at Charlie's' is a reference to a nightclub and lyrically, the song does

seem to allude to trying to catch the eye of some unknown female. Musically it has all the new wave power pop elements you would expect. The chorus is quite catchy, and there are even directions from Orzabal along the way, telling the listener when the good bit is arriving and thanking us at the end.

'Only the Best' (Roland Orzabal, Pauline Moore)

This is an early co-write with Pauline Moore, who was not a member of Graduate, but an associate of the band. In an interview on the *Graham Norton Show* on Virgin Radio at the time of the release of *The Tipping Point*, Roland referenced getting guitar lessons from 'a woman called Pauline'. It is one of the stronger of the unreleased tracks and had the potential to be a single, showing real development in Orzabal's songwriting abilities, although there is no sign of the shift inspired by the Janov teachings that shaped his writing over the next part of his career.

'Think of Me' (Roland Orzabal)

This is a gentle piano-led number and it is a departure for the band. Its influences seem to be far removed from those on the first album with a more AOR, American sound. The piano sounds a bit like the theme from US sitcom *Cheers*.

'Happens So Fast' (Curt Smith, Roland Orzabal, Glenn Tommey)

This is another song that has the feeling of a quiz show theme. It also marked the first time a song co-written by Curt and Roland was released, with the band's producer Glenn Tommey the third credited writer.

'No Second Troy (Alias Sam)' (Roland Orzabal)

It's another Americanised AOR-style song and it marked a more mature sound for the band. If released at the time, it would have been a departure from previous releases, with the piano arrangement carry the song to a chorus which is aimed at a more substantial audience, recalling bands like Wings. It is interesting to view this song as a developmental step in Roland's songwriting. It showed that his influences were slowly being drawn from different perspectives and not just the new wave bands that featured heavily on the debut album.

Stand Alone Singles, B-sides, EPs and Other Contemporary Tracks

Most of the songs that the band recorded with the intention for them to be released have been included in the expanded version of *Acting My Age*, but a few further tracks can be found on YouTube. The *Memories Fade* website also makes reference to other contemporary tracks, such as a Joe Jackson cover of 'I'm the Man' as well as an original Orzabal song called 'White Papers'.

'Mad One' (Roland Orzabal)
Highest chart places: UK: did not chart
In July 1979, Graduate spent three days in Bath's Crescent Studios. During this session, 'Mad One' and 'Somebody Put Out the Fire' were recorded. This is a curious single release that predates the *Acting My Age* album and it never made it to the finished album that came out in 1980. This standalone single was released in 1979 on Blue Hat Records. A limited number of copies were released, making it one of the rarest songs in the Tears For Fears-related back catalogue. It is a tongue-in-cheek, novelty song that was purportedly written to promote a local businessman (Tony Hill) who was something of an eccentric. The lyrics ask whether or not 'he's mad one', the title coming from his 'mad one' car registration plate. The percussion and bassline are a very primitive take on a Giorgio Moroder-style high-energy track and the keyboard sound is reminiscent of what could be heard on Graduate's debut album. The melody has a lullaby or nursery rhyme quality to it. Despite the use of the word mad in the title, it bears no relation to 'Mad World' as some have previously thought, the confusion steming from an incorrect listing on an early Tears For Fears discography.

'Somebody Put Out the Fire' (Roland Orzabal)
Fans of Tears For Fears working their way back through the back catalogue to this one will no doubt be thrown by the Ceilidh-style of this song, with a violin-led folky opening almost morphing into an ELO-style number. This was one of the band's oldest songs and is the only Graduate song to feature John Baker on lead vocals. It was the B-side of 'Mad One' and it had been a part of Graduate's repertoire as early as 1977 – before Curt joined the band. This song harks back to the more folk-inspired sound of the original Orzabal and Baker partnership.

'Me or You' (Roland Orzabal, Curt Smith) (Unreleased Demo)
Unreleased but available on YouTube is this Curt Smith co-write in which he was the lead vocalist. It starts with a dreamy keyboard part before a guitar riff takes hold, acting as the hook throughout the song. It's difficult to make out the lyrics, but it clearly had some potential to have been used at a later date.

The Hurting

Personnel:
Curt Smith: vocals, bass, keyboards
Roland Orzabal: vocals, guitar, keyboards, rhythm programming
Manny Elias: drumming, rhythm programming
Ian Stanley: keyboard programming, computer Programming
Chris Hughes: rhythm Programming, tuned percussion, conducting
Ross Cullum: jazz High, dynamic toggle
Mel Collins: saxophones
Phil Palmer: Palmer picking
Caroline Orzabal: backing vocals
Dave Bates: A&R coordination
Record label: Phonogram/Mercury
Recorded by Chris Hughes and Ross Callum
Release Date: March 1983
Highest Chart Placings: UK: 1, US: 73
Run Time: 41.39

After leaving Graduate in 1981, Roland and Curt set about writing songs for their next project. They wrote demos initially as History of Headaches, having considered other band names, such as Ideas as Opiates and The Upside Down Clinic for their new project.

Their eventual choice of name, Tears For Fears, was inspired by the ideas of Dr Arthur Janov, whose books the *Prisoners of Pain* and *The Primal Scream* had been a stimulus for the pair as they reflected on their childhoods and plotted their next moves. One of Janov's ideas was that 'tears as a replacement for fears' can help address traumatic memories. It was Curt that came up with the name Tears For Fears based on his understanding of Janov, while Roland Orzabal has often been quoted as saying that the band 'wanted to get rich, get famous and get (Primal) therapy'.

The pair were introduced to Janov by a guitar teacher called Pauline Moore, who had also co-written the song 'Only the Best' with Roland Orzabal for Graduate. In an interview in 2022 with Graham Norton on *Virgin Radio*, Orzabal said: 'She was a bit of a hippie. She put an advert in Walcot Street newsagents offering free guitar lessons to delinquent young men'.

Much of the debut album was crafted around these teachings. Some of the chapters of the books were used as song titles. This emphasis on Janov's work suggests that *The Hurting* is something of a concept album and given the themes running through the tracks, it is hard to discount that idea and it's a very fragile album emotionally because of these influences. However, Orzabal and Smith would move away from these philosophies in due course. When they met Janov in the mid-eighties after the band had experienced global chart success and the pair were left disappointed by the meeting. He had supposedly only made contact with the band because he wanted them to write *Primal*

Scream: The Musical. 'We thought he was this cerebral genius, but he just wanted to become big', Curt said of the meeting in the same *Virgin Radio* interview in 2022.

Having found a concept, the sound of the album then became important and a meeting with Ian Stanley was significant in the band's development. Stanley claimed that they met at a Graduate gig, while the band's *Scenes from the Big Chair* documentary claims it was at a vegetarian disco in Bath. Whatever way they met, it was positive for all concerned, with Stanley hearing encouraging things about the pair and wanting to work with them. As a result, the process of working with Stanley in his home studio was not too problematic; it was only when they later worked with name producers in bigger studios that the problems began. Stanley introduced the band to much of the musical technology of the day and they set about recording the first Tears For Fears demos. Roland and Curt's first offering as Tears For Fears was to be 18 months in the making.

Curt Smith, talking to *Super Deluxe Edition's* Paul Sinclair, said of Stanley's involvement: 'Ian was a big part of the initial phase of *The Hurting*, but wasn't as involved in the final recording process. He played a more pivotal role during the recording of *Songs from the Big Chair*. Having said that, he was the person that taught us the nuts and bolts of technology and recording'.

The band were snapped up pretty quickly by their label on the strength of these early demos with A&R man David Bates signing them initially on a 'singles only' deal for Phonogram.

The album sessions set the tone for how the band would record future albums, with delays and changes in the production chair. They worked hard to get the takes right; it was a process that often-brought Curt to his knees. The initial sessions for *The Hurting* with Mike Howlett didn't work out, so he was replaced. It was felt that his contributions were making the album sound too commercial and that he smothered everything in echo and reverb – versions of these initial sessions can be found on the deluxe box set editions. Tensions between the band and the producer also surfaced, especially after he reported the band to the record company for being 'difficult'. David Lloyd, who produced an early version of 'Suffer the Children', was unavailable as he was recording Peter Gabriel's fourth album, so Chris Hughes and Ross Cullum were chosen to take over the recording of the album. Hughes was introduced to Orzabal and Smith through Dave Bates, a friend of Hughes', the producer having originally come to prominence as Merrick (one of the two drummers) in Adam & the Ants. His production credits at the time had included the Liverpool band, Dalek I Love You.

Hughes recalled how he met the band for the first time in an interview in 2015, with Chris Williams at the Red Bull Music Academy:

I just happened to be in the offices when there was a phone call between David Bates and Roland from the band. David said, 'Listen. Why don't you speak to him? See what concerns him and what his issues are.' I had a conversation with him, having never met him.

Fast forward sometime later, when they were trying to put together who might produce the album, Roland allegedly said, 'I'd like to work with that guy I spoke to on the phone.' I was living in London, and they were living in the West Country in England. I caught a train down there, and I met them. We chatted and we got on OK. Fairly soon after that, we came to London and recorded a track called 'Mad World.' So, this was the start of our working relationship. This was either in late 1981 or early 1982.

The process of recording for the album was not as easy as the quick turnaround seems to suggest. The democratic nature of their previous band, in comparison, now made it easier for Orzabal and Smith to get their say in the creative process with this new project. Indeed, the fact that they were no longer touring was a positive step for Orzabal's songwriting process who again took on the main songwriter role in a band, this time, he was more confident to explore his feelings. Roland Orzabal told *The Creative Independent* website when he was previewing 2022's *The Tipping Point*.

It was becoming legitimate to talk about what was going on inside you because it's important. I found that this was a turning point for me —a tipping point, you might say —and all of a sudden, my songs just became way better. If you look at the songs on the Graduate album, which are pretty bad, compared to a song like 'Mad World', it's like a different writer. It's a different person. It's coming from a different part of you. It's coming from your soul. And once you tap into your soul, you are tapping into this huge, huge ocean of possibilities. And at that point, you cannot even claim it as your own.

A considerable influence was the number of synth-orientated acts that emerged in the early part of the decade. While some bands sported vivid colours and images, groups like Joy Division and Echo and the Bunnymen allowed acts like Tears For Fears to wear black and sport a more melancholic image, with Orzabal's writing reflecting changes in the music industry at the time. Depeche Mode, Human League, OMD, and Soft Cell had all begun using the technology of the day, with synthesisers the instrument of choice. Gary Numan's hit 'Are Friend's Electric?' single was a big influence on how Tears For Fears' sound developed. The band have also name-checked Peter Gabriel's third album, David Byrne & Brian Eno's *My Life in the Book of Ghosts*, and Dalek I Love You as other pivotal bands and records. Orzabal has stated that 'what they came up with was a kind of adolescent, fragile, distilled version of those band. The combination of the technology at our disposal — drum machines, synthesizers — plus Janov's theories and philosophy; that was the birth of Tears For Fears,' Orzabal told *The Creative Independent* in 2022.

The balance of acoustic and electronic instrumentation can be explained because Orzabal wrote mainly on his acoustic guitar with Ian Stanley at his 8-track studio. This explains why the album has held up so well after all these years when other music from the era has dated badly.

The Hurting didn't get the critical praise that it deserved at the time. *Rolling Stone* for instance, was not enthusiastic. The more high-minded influences of Janov led to the band being dismissed as being pretentious, while the raw, emotional nature of the lyrics was contradictory to the more hedonistic attitudes that prevailed in the 80s. The *NME*, who once dismissed them as 'Joy Division for weenies', were reticent to acknowledge the album's quality. Gavin Martin's *NME* review in 1983 is indicative of the magazine's point of view:

The music is just the sort of doom-laden dross you'd expect from the lyrics: rehashed and reheated hollow doom with a bit of Ultravox here, diluted Joy Division poured everywhere, and the title track sounding suspiciously like one of the old pompous outfits with a swelter of Mellotrons – Barclay James Harvest perchance?

It is an album for which fans of the band still have high regard, although *MOJO* magazine did ask this question when it was re-released in December 2013:

Has there ever been a more thoroughly miserable mainstream pop album than *The Hurting*? Even when it is up-tempo, it is sombre, and at its most musically adventurous, in the cavernous minimalism of 'Ideas as Opiates' and gnarly dissonances of 'The Prisoner', it's unbearably bereft, but in essence, it was pop.

Its legacy still lives on, having been sampled by several modern-day hip-hop artists. The album did not sell well in the US initially, but its renown has increased over the years as songs have been used on film soundtracks and as samples on songs from other artists.

The book *Mad World: An Oral History of New Wave Artists and Songs that Defined the 1980s* described *The Hurting* as a 'monochromatic expression of resentment and anxiety'.

Roland Orzabal looks back at his teenage self: 'Thank God he was introverted, depressed, I'm not quite sure what else. It was all those raw emotions that went into that album. It made it a special record'.

If ever an album cover was reflective of the contents within, then it is *The Hurting*. The UK sleeve was inspired by the idea that the child is a victim. According to Orzabal in an interview with *Amazon Music in 2022*, the idea for the composition of the cover may have come from an NSPCC advert that was around at the time. The blank background and the image of the boy have become iconic, the boy in question being Curt Smith's neighbour Gebbie Serafin-Jaeger in Bath. Smith revealed in the same interview with *Amazon*

Music, that he is Facebook friends with the grown-up Gebbie. In the US, a different cover was used, which has become known to collectors as the 'Duck Pond' cover – the image is similar to the one used on the 'Mad World' single. It was felt by the US record company that the sleeve of a solitary, sobbing child might not be commercial enough.

Super Deluxe Editions
To mark the 30th anniversary in 2013, the album was remastered and released in both a two-disc 'Deluxe Expanded Edition' and a four-disc (3CD+1DVD) 'Super Deluxe Edition'. These versions set the template for other box sets that have been released for *Songs from the Big Chair* and *The Seeds of Love*. Disc one contains the original album. On disc two, there are several different versions of single releases, extended mixes, and B-sides. Disc three is a disc of live versions of the album taken from BBC Radio 1 'Peel Sessions' and 'Jensen Sessions'. The final disc is a live DVD of the 1983 video release *In My Mind's Eye (Live at Hammersmith Odeon)*, which features several tracks from *The Hurting*, as well as songs that would appear on *Songs from the Big Chair*, such as 'Mother's Talk', 'We Are Broken' and 'Head Over Heels'. The box set comes with a detailed booklet written by Paul Sinclair of Super Deluxe Edition and a reproduction of the On the Road tour programme.

'The Hurting' (Roland Orzabal)
The title track is a mission statement from the band. It suggests that Tears For Fears were going to be a weightier proposition than Graduate, both lyrically and musically. The lyrics were more powerful than anything Orzabal had written before. Musically the style had shifted too. Orzabal said this about the song in the liner notes of the 2013 re-release of the album:

Writing the title track was a strange piece of psychic osmosis. Curt had been to see a band from Bristol called Electric Guitars and was describing their sound to me; I had an acoustic guitar in my hand at the time and played him what he was describing: that's how 'The Hurting' was written, and we knew for a long time it was the right name for our first album.

The sparse drums are a portent of the band's early sound. Peter Gabriel's 'Intruder' may well have been an inspiration. Especially the rhythmic elements. The guitar riffs have certain similarities and both 'Intruder' and 'The Hurting' are the opening tracks of their respective albums. There are also synth-line screams in both songs. Curt and Roland are listed as the singers on this one, but Roland does the majority of the work, with Curt appearing with the 'is it a horrific dream' line throughout the song. It's the moment that Orzabal can be seen to have finally found his voice as a singer and songwriter.

In recent years the band have become used to artists sampling songs from the album, and this was the first song to be used elsewhere. A half-speed sample of the drum intro used on the Band-Aid charity single 'Do They Know It's Christmas.' This was done without the band's knowledge and it was only late in the day that they were informed by the song's co-writer, Midge Ure, that the element had been used.

'Mad World' (Roland Orzabal)
Highest chart places: UK: 3

Given that the band had initially been signed only on a singles-only deal in the UK, there was pressure to deliver a hit. This was more pronounced, especially given the failure of the first singles 'Suffer the Children' and 'Pale Shelter (You Don't Give Me Love)' when they were first released. The band's A&R man, Dave Bates' belief in the band had not wavered and he was still pushing the record label for the album deal. But their first big hit was almost the one that got away. They set out to record new tracks that were potentially going to be used as the B-side of 'Pale Shelter (You Don't Give Me Love)' and they initially dismissed 'Mad World' as nothing more than a B-side. That was until the intervention of Bates, who suggested that the song was a potential single. Even though it was strong, it was not anticipated that it would become the hit that it became with the idea being to put it out it to gain some attention and build from there. When it was released in October 1982, it reached number three in the UK charts and stayed in the charts for 18 weeks. This single version was the one that appeared on the album combined with a slightly longer, sharper mix known as 'Mad World (World Remix)', which was part of a 7-inch double pack. This multi formatting helped to prolong the song's chart life.

Quoted in the *NME* in November 1982, even Orzabal was surprised by the success of the song:

> I just don't know who is buying it. We had support from the DJs who've been playing our stuff for some time, but the way all the other DJs picked it up immediately was totally unexpected.

The idea for the song came to Orzabal when he was living in a two-bedroom flat above a pizza restaurant in Bath. His then-girlfriend (later his wife), Caroline, had three jobs to support the pair. That allowed Orzabal to sit at home with his guitar and 'sort of sing this melancholia all day and feel sorry for myself'. Lyrically one of the inspirations could have been Paul Simon's 'Still Crazy After all These Years', a song that Orzabal said to *Entertainment Weekly* in 1993, was one that he'd wished he had written. 'There's such a calm, cool, philosophical outlook in that song, a kind of acceptance that things aren't perfect. It's a state I'd like to get to'. Both songs are reflective and have the narrator looking out through a window and watching the world go by.
On 'Mad World' Orzabal is sitting at his bedroom window, failing to understand people's 9 to 5 existences, although in the liner notes for the album, he

pointed out: 'Not that Bath is very mad – I should have called it 'Bourgeois World'.

Another inspiration came from Dalek I Love You, the band that producer Hughes had been associated with. They had a lyric in a song that went 'I believe the world's gone mad', about which in an interview with *The Guardian's* Dave Simpson in 2013, Orzabal saying that the song mirrored 'his feelings of alienation from the rat race'.

The opening percussive sound that announces the song is hugely recognisable. The bass synth was inspired by Duran Duran's 'Girls on Film'. Orzabal said in the same interview:

I just thought: 'I'm going to have a crack at something like that.' I did and ended up with 'Mad World.' It sounded pretty awful on guitar, though, with just me singing. However, we were fortunate enough to be given an opportunity by a guy called Ian Stanley to go to his very big house and muck about on his synthesizer. Ian became our keyboard player and he had a drum machine, too. All we needed was someone who knew how to work it. Eventually, we made the first demo of 'Mad World' still with me singing.

Curt Smith was the singer on the final release and he was to become the lucky mascot when it came to singing the hits, as Orzabal explained to *GQ* in 2022:

Curt went in and did the vocal, it's like fuckin' hell, night and day. I am under no illusions that the two biggest songs in our catalogue, and the biggest earners for me, are 'Mad World' and 'Everybody Wants to Rule the World,' and that's Curt singing them. He does something to a song, and we are kind of spoiled for choice as to who sings what.

It is another Janov-influenced song that suggests that dreams of intense experiences such as death are the best at releasing tension. It's not a suicide reference as it is sometimes believed, being merely derived from a paragraph about bad dreams sucking away the negative. The song is minimalist yet bold.

There's a line in the song that references a Halargian world. This relates to a fictional planet which was an in-joke within the band about 'being so far off the map that you're from planet Halarge', from a comment made by either producer Ross Cullum or Chris Hughes. Some cover versions have therefore changed the line 'Enlarging your world...' the Gary Jules cover in particular. There have even been references to 'illogical world', and 'raunchy young world'.

The video for the single was directed by Clive Richardson and was shot at Knebworth Country Park, Hertfordshire, England, the location used for Smith looking out on the world through the window. The video is notable for the curious interpretive dance by Orzabal. This was no aberration on the part of the songwriter, as he was known to do this in the recording studio to show his pleasure that the process was going well. The band also bussed in friends and family from Bath for the shoot – the woman having the birthday party in the video is Curt Smith's mum.

There have been suggestions that the verse of 'Mad World' has similarities to Cat Steven's 'Matthew & Son'. Stevens has even referred to this in a concert on his 2016 tour when he sang the lyrics 'I think it's kind of funny, I think it's kind of strange, yes, I think it's kind of funny, that this sounds the same'.

The song has famously had a second life beyond the confines of 'The Hurting'. Gary Jules and Michael Andrews adapted the song for the piano and slowed it down, becoming part of the soundtrack for the 2001 movie *Donnie Darko*, later (in 2003) reaching the number one slot in the UK, charting higher than the band's version.

The band have arranged the song in numerous ways down the years to perform it live; they've even tried it in the Andrews/Jules style, most notably, on BBC Radio 2's *Piano Room* sessions in February 2022. There's also a distinctive version on the *Secret World – Live in Paris* album that updates the arrangement of the song.

'Pale Shelter' (Roland Orzabal)
Highest chart places: UK: 5.

Before the album, this song was released as the band's second single. 'Pale Shelter (You Don't Give Me Love)', failed to chart initially. It was later re-released after the record-buying public were alerted to the band after the success of 'Change' and 'Mad World'. The re-release of 'Pale Shelter' (the band dropped the 'you don't give me love' from the title) gave the band its third top ten hit in the UK.

The original version of 'Pale Shelter' along with 'Suffer the Children', formed part of the demo that got the band signed. Written by Orzabal and sung by bassist Smith, the extended introduction has an acoustic guitar that is struck on the beat, underpinned by synth bass. The beginning of the original 1982 single has a backwards vocal over the intro that says: 'The sickness in the system is an amplification of the sickness in the individual', removed for the album version. There would be a further release of the song in 1985 to cash in on the success of *Songs from the Big Chair*, which would reach number 73 in the UK.

It's another song that mines the Janov texts. It is about the pain and insecurity that stems from not receiving enough affection from parents: 'I'm calling you/I'm calling you/I asked for more and more/ How can I be sure/ When you don't give me love/ You gave me pale shelter'.

Roland Orzabal said in an interview with *Record Mirror* in November 1982 that the inspiration for the song came from 'playing two chords for weeks and weeks, then one morning I woke up and sang the tune and the words, just like that. Then another day, I was flicking through an art book and came across 'Pale Shelter Scene' by Henry Moore, so that wrapped up everything nicely'. The painting shows Londoners taking sanctuary in the underground during World War II.

Having recorded the early version with Mike Howlett, 'Pale Shelter' was difficult to record, reducing Curt's to tears due to the number of takes it took to get right.

The song has a bizarre video shot in Los Angeles and it's another song that has been repurposed by other artists, with The Weeknd, for instance, sampling it for their synth disco-house track called 'Secrets'.

'Ideas as Opiates' (Roland Orzabal)

This song was originally released as the B-side to the 'Mad World' single and was later re-recorded for inclusion on the album. The title is taken from a chapter in *Prisoners of Pain* by Arthur Janov, which discusses religion being the opiate of the masses. Orzabal explained in the remastered album's (1999) liner notes:

It's a reference to people's mindsets, the way that the ego can suppress so much nasty information about oneself – the gentle way that the mind can fool oneself into thinking everything is great.

Roland sings this sparsely arranged tune, which features just a piano, synth percussion and a saxophone. Its repetitive loop has the feeling of a mantra, while the track itself feels like a segue from one part of the album to the next. The saxophone at the end relieves the sparseness of the song and is played superlatively by Mel Collins (King Crimson, The Rolling Stones). This saxophone part is expanded upon for the primarily instrumental B-side version 'Saxophones as Opiates' (which appears on the reverse of the expanded single versions of 'Mad World').

It's another song that's inspired another artist, Drake sampling it for his 2009 song 'Lust for Life'.

'Memories Fade' (Roland Orzabal)

This is one of the strongest songs on the album and remains a live favourite. Roland Orzabal's powerful vocal dominates and shows his developing songcraft. It was written on Ian Stanley's JP4 synth using one of the pre-set sounds giving it the distinctive keyboard motif that runs through the song, providing a sort of wah-wah effect. There is more saxophone – this time at the song's end. It's the longest track and it's the song that holds the album together. On the vinyl version, it was the closing track for side one. It feels like it is in the right place on the CD release too, siting in the middle of the album alongside 'Suffer the Children'. Its place on the album shows the power of sequencing and how a narrative can be built across a collection of songs. Musically it has a haunting arrangement – the last of the brooding songs on side one. The songs that follow are still lyrically dense, but the arrangements are more upbeat.

It's another song that has been sampled by another generation of artists. Kanye West used it for his song 'Coldest Winter' in 2008, which he'd written about the death of his mother. When Tears For Fears played 'Memories Fade' at a gig after Kanye's version, the nanny for Curt's then young children told him how wonderful it is that they had sampled a Kanye song. Curt Smith expressed his feelings about the reinterpretations to *Stereogum* in 2022:

> I always think, if people repurpose what we do, then I'm kind of fine with it. I find it interesting to hear someone else's interpretation of what we do. It's when someone copies what you've done and tries to do what you did; it's sort of boring.

'Suffer the Children' (Roland Orzabal)
Highest chart places: UK: 53
This was the band's first single and another of the songs that formed part of the demo that got the band signed with David Lord. Richard Zuckerman, who was an A&R guy at Pye Records and who had played a part in getting Graduate signed, funded the initial recording.

It was one of the band's first experiments with synths. The song was released as the debut single in November 1981, failing to chart, despite being championed by Radio 1 DJ Peter Powell. The B-side was 'Wino'. The later release reached 53 in the charts, while a remixed version also appears on the 12-inch of 'Mad World'. It was a UK-only release and was issued on both 7' and 12' vinyl.

'Suffer the Children' is another Janov-inspired track that deals with the loneliness that a child feels because of his or her absent parents and this notion is also represented in the album's cover. Orzabal explained in the liner notes of the 1999 remastered album. 'We really thought that children were born innocent and good and holy ... When you've got kids of your own, you realize how bloody difficult it is. But it's that kind of thing – saying look at what you're doing with your child.'

Andy Marsden, from Graduate, plays the drums on the original recording of the song. The original has a choral vocal over the intro, which was taken out for the album version. The electronic bassline sounds a bit like OMD's 'Enola Gay', a band that was one of the early influences for Tears For Fears.

The song has been given a new lease of life on the band's 2022, *Tipping Point* World Tour and it has been reinterpreted as a song for a female vocal. The band's backing singers, Carina Round (the early US dates) and Lauren Evans (later US and UK dates) have both highlighted the qualities of the song with their vocal prowess. Both versions have been well received by the fans and the band members when performed live. Great versions from both singers can be found on YouTube.

'Watch Me Bleed' (Roland Orzabal)
This song highlights the contrasts contained within the sound of the album. The song opens with a treated guitar riff that acts as the hook, while the strummed acoustic guitar is the dominant part of the song. Other guitars come

and go. Guitar stabs are present, a style that crops up at various points across the album, while a discreet synth part pulls it all together. There is a reference to the title of the album in the lyrics 'well we've denied the hurting'. The acoustic guitar highlights the fact that a lot of the album was written on that instrument and it's powerfully sung by Roland. This is an upbeat song with lyrics that do not match the vibrant nature of the track but do fit the sonic and lyrical themes of the album.

'Change' (Roland Orzabal)
Highest chart places: UK: 4, US: 73.
Another hit and another Curt vocal. This was the follow-up single of 'Mad World', also landing in the UK top ten when it was released in January 1983. The big draw is the captivating marimba part in the intro, making it one of the catchiest, hookiest numbers on the album. Originally written by Orzabal for his wife Caroline to sing, Curt heard the demo and liked it, suggesting that it should go on the album. It was a song that Orzabal had not thought of as being a Tears For Fears song, as he explained to the magazine *One Two Testing* in October 1984:

The riff came first for 'Change'. Actually, I wasn't thinking of using 'Change', because I thought at the time it was too poppy, too simple, just yuk. Anyway, the riff translates on a lot of instruments... I decided to do it on a marimba sound because I didn't like the riff. If I don't like a riff, I always put it on marimbas. Rule number one: if the riff's no good, put it on marimbas! Marimbas are a lovely sound, everyone uses 'em. That was done on a Prophet, but it's quite easy to play on real marimbas, believe me. All your left hand is doing is offbeat. We did it with real marimbas live, but you couldn't hear them. Forget it.

There are multiple versions knocking around that have been released in various formats down the years. The deluxe and expanded editions of the album do a good job of collating these. The UK cassette version of *The Hurting* as well as certain copies of the 'Change' 12-inch single contained 'Change (New Version)', although this is an early version of the song from the Mike Howlett sessions, which the band did not like. It is easy to see why; it has an annoying rhythm track that gets in the way of the melody and there are also different lyrics on that version. The song is all the better for the later revisions.

The video is set in a tower block with Curt in a lift surrounded by strangely dressed Japanese figures in masks. We also get Roland with a steel guitar and more of his dancing.

'The Prisoner' (Roland Orzabal)
This is quite experimental within the running order of the album. It's a forerunner to the improvisations and styles that they would employ for future

B-sides. A version of this appears on the second pre-album single 'Pale Shelter (You Don't Give Me Love)' and also on the 1985 re-release of that single. Again, there are hints of Peter Gabriel's 'Intruder'. It was no doubt this song that raised the ire of *NME*'s Gavin Martin in his sniffy review, he referred to the 'swelter of Mellotrons'. Amongst the new technology, the band found a use for an instrument that was a precursor for the modern synth and the Mellotron choir is used to good effect as a counterpoint to Smith's haunting vocal.

'Start of the Breakdown' (Roland Orzabal)
The album closer was directly influenced by Orzabal's childhood, particularly the illness that left his father semi-bedridden. He has said in the liner notes for deluxe 'It was a reference to my father, who had a nervous breakdown. 'Dry skin flakes when there's ice in the veins...' He had arterial sclerosis, and the 'breakdown' is a nervous one.' Set against these lyrics is a musical arrangement that opens with a distinctive motif. The single piano chords build tension in the melody. There is a busy bassline that seems to conflict with the main melody, but it works quite well. There are times that there is so much going on musically that you do not notice the subject matter. The song builds to a satisfying musical climax.

Stand Alone Singles, B-sides, EPs and Other Contemporary Tracks
There aren't many other songs to be found from this period. A majority of the songs that were released as B-sides were alternative versions of songs that appeared on *The Hurting*. Whether 'The Way You Are' marks the end of *The Hurting* or the start of *Songs from the Big Chair* period is arguable. It is included here for context. It can be found on the band's B-sides and rarities collection, *Saturnine Martial & Lunatic*. It is also on the deluxe box set for *Songs from the Big Chair.*

'Saxophones as Opiates' (Roland Orzabal)
This was on the 12-inch version of 'Mad World' and it's a chilled-out saxophone-driven version of 'Ideas as Opiates'. It's an instrumental apart from a brief vocal from Orzabal singing 'we don't care'. It was surprisingly left off the deluxe and super deluxe versions of *'The Hurting*, the band's reason for vetoing it was because they think this version is 'cheesy'.

'We Are Broken' (Roland Orzabal)
The B-side of the 1983 'Pale Shelter' (New Single Version). 'We Are Broken' is a more experimental version of a song that would appear on the band's second album, simply called 'Broken', where a studio cut and live version bookend 'Head Over Heels'. This version is more electronic in style, almost demo-like and it was playing the song live on the band's first few tours that led to 'Broken/Head Over Heels' emerging. The riff is recognisable from later

versions, while the bassline is synthesised. The synth motif that appears on 'Head Over Heels' is still present, and so too is the guitar break, which is less polished in this form.

'The Conflict' (Roland Orzabal, Curt Smith, Ian Stanley)

This was the B-side of 'Change', with minimal vocals and a percussive beat running through the track. It's experimental but marks an interesting snapshot of the evolution of the band's sound, in that it's not a million miles away from 'The Way You Are'. It's very much a B-side.

'Wino' (Roland Orzabal)

A B-side of both the 1983 and 1985 (re)release of Pale Shelter. This is directly about Orzabal's relationship with his father, though it feels like a demo recording – no more than guitar and vocals, making it something of a departure from the band's then sound. It's an emotionally raw song that depicts his father as a pathetic loser who doesn't want to do anything but drink and smoke all day, happy to die slowly from his addictions. When he was interviewed by *Super Deluxe Edition's* Paul Sinclair about the inclusion of the song on the deluxe edition releases of *The Hurting*, Orzabal simply answered: 'Oh dear. Can we take that one off?'

'The Way You Are' (Manny Elias, Roland Orzabal, Curt Smith, Ian Stanley)

Highest chart places: UK: 24.

The wayward son of the Tears For Fears singles back catalogue finally made it onto a compilation with the release of *Saturnine Martial & Lunatic* in 1996. Despite being a hit single, it was omitted from the main compilation albums *Tears Roll Down* and *Rule the World*. Given the band's antipathy towards it, it's not difficult to work out why it has been marooned on that collection. It's never likely to rear its head again on any future hits compilations either,

It was a song that drew a veil over the first phase of the band. It's largely been forgotten by the band, but it did act as a catalyst for their next direction. It has a curious rhythm track that is very bold for a single – perhaps better placed as one of their artier B-sides. Orzabal has claimed it was their attempt at trying to take on Japan and David Sylvian's brand of electro-pop-funk and as a result, it features one of the band's first forays into sampling. The song is heavily programmed using sounds and textures rather than melody. It was the last time that Ross Cullum was involved in the production of a Tears For Fears song.

Released in November 1983, eight months after the debut album, the song was a stepping stone between *The Hurting* and *Songs from the Big Chair*. It's something of a departure and demonstrates that the band were right to go back to the drawing board and plan out their next album from scratch. It was released in the UK (not in the US) as a single with an extended twelve-inch mix, which rewarded the band with an appearance on BBC's *Top of the Pops*.

The band considered it a misstep, something that the Orzabal acknowledges in the sleeve notes of the rarities compilation, suggesting it was 'the point at which we realised we had to change direction'.

What is interesting about the song, with the benefit of decades of hindsight, is that the structure of the song could be seen as a template for 'Shout'. The chorus of both 'Shout' and 'The Way You Are' start each song. As an experiment, the song might not have worked for the band, but it may have led them to produce material that was more commercial and less arty. The success of the *Songs from the Big Chair* album could be seen as evidence of that. They had similar issues getting 'Mother's Talk' right, so these missteps changed the band's direction for the better.

Songs from the Big Chair

Personnel:
Roland Orzabal: guitar, keyboards, vocals, grand piano, bass synth, LinnDrum programming
Curt Smith: bass guitar, vocals, bass synth
Ian Stanley: keyboards, LinnDrum programming, arrangements
Manny Elias: drums, drum arrangement
Sandy McLelland: backing vocals
Chris Hughes: drums, LinnDrum, MIDI programming
Jerry Marotta: percussion, saxophone arrangement
Will Gregory: saxophone solos
Mel Collins: saxophone
Andy Davis: grand piano
Neil Taylor: guitar
Stevie Lange: backing vocals
Annie McCaig: backing vocals
Marilyn Davis: backing vocals
Record label: Phonogram/Mercury
Recorded: Chris Hughes and Dave Bascombe
Release Date: 25th February 1985
Highest Chart Placings: UK: 2, US: 1
Run Time: 41:52

It is reductive to say that Tears For Fears are an 80s band as, despite the infrequency of their releases, they have existed as a band for over four decades. However, those that only have a passing interest in their output will point to the songs on this album as 'typical' Tears For Fears. Roland Orzabal has noted that when new albums in more recent decades have been released, they have largely been ignored beyond the fanbase, but the renewed focus of the band in the media has kick-started interest in the band's back catalogue. Most people will have heard and seen these songs on the radio, in film and commercials. If a film wants that shorthand to define the age, the opening arpeggio of 'Everyone Wants to Rule the World' and the huge sound of 'Shout' will do that in an instant. *Songs from the Big Chair* is an era-defining album, hence the labelling of Tears For Fears as the archetypical 80s band.

Speaking to Paul Lester of *Record Collector* in 2014, Orzabal claimed that the album was a bit of a different beast from its predecessor:

It only had eight tracks on it. 'Head over Heels' had been knocking around for a while. 'The Working Hour 'we'd had since 1983. Then there's 'Broken', which appears twice (the second time in live form). I couldn't take *Big Chair* seriously. It didn't have the continuity of 'The Hurting' and that's why I suggested we call it *Songs from* ... something ... because to me, it was just a collection of songs.

David Bates says that the inspiration for the title may have come from a big leather chair that was in Ian Stanley's house-cum-studio where the bulk of the album was recorded. The 'big chair' in question was where members of the band would fall asleep during studio downtime. In fact, the big chair was also mooted as a potential front cover image.

It is worth noting the run time of the tracks. The band was already moving beyond three-minute pop songs and morphing from introspective shoegazing musicians to a band that were equipped for the bigger arenas that followed the album's release. This was still pop music, but it was all the more progressive in sound and approach.

If *The Hurting* had set a template for difficult recording processes, then in its early stages, the follow-up was no less problematic. The single release for 'The Way You Are', a stop-gap between albums, and the early versions of 'Mother's Talk' stalled their progress a little. The tone of the new track, 'Mother's Talk', was more muscular than their previous singles. The initial video showed that things had changed in the band, with then clad in black, brandishing guitars. This song was written before the bulk of the recording for *Songs from the Big Chair* and it landed at number 14 on the UK singles charts – a relative failure following the success of the singles from *The Hurting*. But these missteps helped to put the band back on track to complete the album in the manner that it turned out.

Producer Chris Hughes was one of the main players, alongside Ian Stanley and the band, in getting the album finished. Hughes was not on board at the start, as it seemed that the band wanted to produce themselves. They had begun recording in 1984 at Ian Stanley's home studio without Hughes, but when he was finally brought on board, he was fired several times whenever they would disagree about something, although he claims that was fired more during the recording sessions for *The Seeds of Love*.

Songs from the Big Chair came out in the age of the vinyl record, and CDs were only beginning to gain their prominence. Looking at the running order and listening to the album as a whole, it is clear that the band was making a vinyl album, with sides A and B having certain characteristics. It makes sense to open with 'Shout' and for 'Mother's Talk' to close side A, while bookending 'Broken' and 'Head over Heels' with 'I Believe' and 'Listen' are quite inspired choices.

It was one of the biggest albums in 1985. So huge, it did enough to knock Michael Jackson's *Thriller* off the top of the charts in the US. It is estimated that today the album has sold over 20 million copies.

The inclusion of classic elements such as lead guitar solos on songs like 'Shout' has meant that the album has not dated like some of its contemporaries and it still stands up sonically today. Even though most of *Songs from the Big Chair* was produced using the technology of the time, instruments like the Prophet-5, DX7, LinnDrum and the Fairlight system made it easy to build up quite sophisticated sounds. This use of technology was the reason for the great leap in sound between albums one and two for the band. Indeed, in 2020, it was given classic album status on the long-running TV documentary series.

The front cover design fits with the theme of the album, but originally it had a more abstract cover; something artier that incorporated squiggles in the style of Miró. This idea was rejected. Today, you could not imagine the album without the black and white picture of the two principal members, Curt and Roland, dressed in their knitwear and budget sports tops. Indeed, the cover art was the antithesis of the glossy new romantic albums of the age.

When interviewed in 2014 by *Record Collector* magazine's Paul Lester, Orzabal said of the cover:

It was iconic, but it was all done on the hoof. We did this photo session, and I looked through the proofs and saw this one picture of me and Curt, with him in a jumper and me wearing a zip-up top owned by Richard Jobson of The Skids, lent to me by Mariella Frostrup, his girlfriend of the time and our press officer at Phonogram. It came together by chance, but it became an 80s icon.

Super Deluxe Editions

It is the second album from the band's back catalogue to be given the 'deluxe edition' and 'super deluxe edition' treatment, and it is a more substantial collection than the one released for *The Hurting*. Disc one has the original album and the B-sides. The second disc has a selection of single versions of the albums and remixes, of which there were plenty during this period. There is also an interview with Curt and Roland recorded at the time. Those discs appear on both the 'deluxe edition' and 'super deluxe edition'. The latter has more discs, with the third containing all the extended mixes and the 12' releases. Disc four has the live tracks taken from BBC Radio 1's Richard Skinner shows, as well as tracks from the Massey Hall gig, which appears in video form on the band's documentary – the full concert can be found on the 2021 Record Store Day release of *Tears For Fears: Live at Massey Hall Toronto, Canada 1985*. Disc five is a DVD containing the 5.1 Mix and 2014 Stereo mixes of the album. The final and sixth disc is another DVD containing the band's documentary *Scenes from the Big Chair*, an interview with producer Chris Hughes, as well as a selection of promo videos from the time. There is also a selection of BBC TV Appearances, including some from *Top of The Pops* and the *Wogan* programmes. The box set comes with a detailed booklet featuring interviews with all the main players in the story of the making of the album and a reproduction of the *Songs from the Big Chair* tour programme.

'Shout' (Roland Orzabal, Ian Stanley)
Highest chart places: UK: 4, US: 1.
This was the band's second single release from the album and the one that shaped their destiny for the next few years. The theme of 'Shout' has been

interpreted as being another Janov-inspired song, but in truth, it's more in keeping with the band's development of a less introspective viewpoint, moving towards broader perspectives, such as politics. It was written at a time when Cold War tensions were on the rise – also part of the inspiration for the song.

'They gave you life/in return you gave them hell' does cover the same ground as songs from *The Hurting*, but this track goes farther than that; it's about using your voice and protesting, but at who and what was open for interpretation.

There was a feeling during the initial sessions that the album was light on potential singles; they needed to come up with a few more. It was one of two songs that were written during the recording of the new album during a period when Orzabal was given time off to write, mid-recording. The original idea came from him messing around with a Talking Heads rhythm track – 'Seen and Not Seen' from *Remain in Light)* – on the LinnDrum and the Prophet-5 synth in his front room, the initial demo being only a chorus.

Everyone liked the looping on the chorus, but the verse took a lot more work. Hughes supposedly gave Stanley and Orzabal an hour to get the song right at one point, but in reality, it took a lot longer than that for it to come together. There was a reluctance on the part of Orzabal to add other verses to the song, with a feeling that the song was going to have an 'All You Need is Love' vibe to it. The original, impassioned vocal was done in a few takes.

They threw in a big guitar solo and keyboard break too. Guitar solos had fallen out of favour in pop music in the 80s, so it's these elements make it less of an 80s song stylistically and give it a more timeless quality.

A lot of the song stems from the drum pattern. The use of the technology at the time led to accusations that Tears For Fears has copied the sound from other sources and there is certainly a nod to Led Zeppelin's 'When the Levee Breaks', a sample that they would utilise to good effect again on *The Tipping Point* album.

The 6:32 running time was way over the ideal length for a single on both sides of the Atlantic. In the UK, the single edit is 4:47 and in the US is 4:06. The fade is less abrupt with the UK release, but it still misses out on the epic climax to the song, which can be heard in all its glory on the album. The band's A&R man Dave Bates was instrumental in the edits, much to the annoyance of the band. They would make their feelings about this decision known elsewhere on the album.

Epic songs demand epic videos, and the outdoor scenes for 'Shout' were filmed at Durdle Door, Dorset, on the south coast of England. Roland and Curt are on the cliff edges shouting out into the distance. This is interspersed with the keyboard and bassist playing the song. We are shown how the song is played in close up, which is great for the bedroom musician. Roland plays his guitar solo on the mountain cliff edge and then it is back in the studio.

There are numerous alternative mixes, which are longer/shorter to satisfy the demands of the record labels and the numerous other formats. As well as the album cut, there are versions with the following additional titles. A Cappella,

Alternative Mix, Alternative Version, Extended Version, Short Version, Single Version, US Single Edit, US Single Version, UK Version/Extended Version, US Dub Version, and the US Remix. These can be heard across the super deluxe edition box sets. The 'Shout (US Remix)' by Steve Thompson and Michael Barbiero was particularly significant in making the song the hit it was in the US.

In the UK, the single peaked at number four and stayed in the top ten for seven weeks. It became the band's sixth UK top 40 hit and it also reached number one on the *Billboard* Hot 100 in August 1985 and remained there for three weeks.

'The Working Hour' (Roland Orzabal, Ian Stanley, Manny Elias)

The sax solo at the start of this song is simply beautiful. There is also stunning instrumentation beneath that recalls the work of the composer Ryuichi Sakamoto, but it is the drumming that propels this piece. The part was written by Manny Elias and it was a song that the band had been working on in rehearsals on the tour that preceded the sessions for *Songs from the Big Chair*. Curiously, on the record, the drum part was played by Peter Gabriel's regular session drummer Jerry Marotta, who wasn't exactly sure why he came in to do the session, given the quality of Elias as a drummer. Ian Stanley has said that Elias had his limitations in the studio, being more effective as a live performer. But quite rightly, Elias gets a songwriting credit for coming up with this part.

The song came together quickly, feeling quite organic and that is why the vibe is more like a band playing live than something that was pieced together in the studio. Producer Hughes, who had been instrumental in creating a lot of the other songs on the album, has said that he sat back and watched the song evolve. There's a great vocal from Orzabal and there is also some fine bass guitar from Smith.

The melody line had been used previously on the song 'When in Love with a Blind Man', which was to become the B-side of 'Head of Over Heels'. That song had been written before 'The Working Hour', starting life as a solo piano piece. However, that first take on the melody was more synthesised, while this updated song had the saxophone as the main feature. 'Saxophone was always part of 'The Working Hour,' because of the riff. The main saxophone riff is extremely important and powerful – it's got that sort of 'crying' quality to it,' Orzabal recalled to *The Sound Bard*.

There is a credit on the song for Stanley. He had the original melody for the chorus and Orzabal suggested a verse that would complement it, although Stanley took some time to be convinced that the two elements would work together.

Lyrically, the 'We are paid by those who learn by our mistakes' is a dig at the record company for putting pressure on the band to follow up and repeat the success of previous singles. Curt pushed for the album to be named after this track, but Roland's idea won out in the end.

Given the calibre of songs it sits alongside, it more than pulls its weight. According to Curt Smith, during the band's Spotify sessions in 2014, it's the band's most requested song, bar the hits. It's a huge fan favourite, but sadly, it didn't make it to the set list of the initial dates of the 2022 tour.

'Everybody Wants to Rule the World' (Roland Orzabal, Ian Stanley, Chris Hughes)
Highest chart places: UK: 2, US: 1.
It's hard to imagine that a song called 'Everyone Wants to Go to War' would have had the same impact as the song that was eventually called 'Everybody Wants to Rule the World'.
That uncertainty may have explained the reluctance of Orzabal to finish the song when it still had that original title. Roland had constantly been playing a little vamp in the studio of the song's initial two chords and on hearing this, Chris Hughes pushed him to finish it off. He also urged them to change the title. Orzabal's wife, Caroline, was a champion of the song too and without these interventions, the song might have ended up as a nice riff without a home.

The distinctive opening two chords formed part of the initial demo. Producers Hughes and Stanley built the song around the chords Orzabal had been messing around with. Hughes then added the shuffle beat and Stanley came up with the distinctive trickle-down keyboard part with Hughes playing the drums. He then transcribed and sequenced them in midi, then a new technology designed for recording and playing back music on digital synthesizers.

This is usually where things get laborious in the process of recording a Tears for fears song. Not with this one: 'Everybody Wants to Rule the World' was so simple and went down so quickly, that it seemed effortless. 'In fact, [considering its status] as a piece of recording history, it's bland as hell', Hughes said of the recording in an interview with *Mix Magazine*.

There are similarities with the bass and percussive beat of Simple Mind's hit 'Waterfront'. The band have owned up to the use of 'Waterfront' parts of the rhythm were programmed using that as a template. British funk act Linx's song 'Throwing Away the Key' was used for the more trebly sound of the rhythm.

In an age when guitar solos were frowned upon, Tears For Fears decided to go against the conventional wisdom and included two – and they are both outstanding. It is claimed that the end solo was nailed in two takes and these have been edited into the solo that we hear on the record. Neil Taylor's playing is genius, that's even without knowing that it was recorded with such ease. Orzabal played the more rhythmic solo earlier in the song. It's an outlier in the Tears For Fears discography, yet it's become their calling card, even though it has an unconventional structure. Despite it being an anthemic MTV-friendly hit, there is no discernible chorus as such.

Because the song came together quite quickly in two weeks, unheard of for Tears For Fears, it meant that the track not have that chance to become overworked. Initially, the band did not consider it as a potential hit record, thinking it was part of the listening journey of the album, which needed a less intense song. Even though it's light and airy, the concept behind the lyrics is quite serious, and while there is no overall meaning, there are a series of arresting couplets. It could be about power in the pollical sphere, it is also about the hierarchy of their record label at the time. One inspiration was that the single version of 'Shout' had to be faded because of its length, so the band again got their own back by highlighting this in the chorus with 'so sad we had to fade it'.

For a song that was deemed to be lightweight, it was just what Dave Bates was crying out for. He wanted a drive-time hit that would push the band in the American markets. He had that and more with the song. The video was also instrumental in the band consolidating their position in America after the release of 'Shout'. It is very American in tone and it chimed well with the times, just as MTV was beginning to be a big thing. In the video, Curt can be seen driving through the desert in an antique mid-1960s Austin-Healey 3000 Mark III convertible sports car painted in British Racing Green. This footage is interspersed with the band of the time playing in a fairly anonymous-looking studio. Any great song backed by strong visuals stood the chance of being successful.

When it was released, 'Everybody Wants to Rule the World' missed out on the number one spot in the UK, stalling at number two. In the US, though, it topped the *Billboard* Hot 100 charts and by 2021 it was Spotify's most streamed song from the entire 80s decade. It has been covered by artists such as Lorde and Robert Glasper, with both finding new and distinctive ways of approaching it. It has even appeared in movie soundtracks such as *Ready Player One* so its appeal shows no sign of diminishing any time soon.

'Mothers Talk' (Roland Orzabal, Ian Stanley)
Highest chart places: UK: 14, US: 27

Having taken something of a misstep with 'The Way We Are' single in late 1983, the band moved on with writing and recording the next album. After the initial sessions in early 1984, the band went into the studio to record 'Mothers Talk' as their next single. The sound was more robust and guitar-led – a step away from the stark minimalism of *The Hurting with* Jeremy Green assigned the role of producer. He had a good pedigree, given he had previously worked with The Pretenders and Terry Hall, but the initial sessions did not work out and Chris Hughes returned as producer. The version of 'Mother's Talk' that appears on the album is a re-recorded version.

The song is the result of several takes. The first attempt was very synth-orientated, but Chris Hughes thought the track would sound great with heavier guitars, while Orzabal disagreed. Displeased, he strummed the guitar angrily, much to the delight of the producer, who realised that this was exactly the sound the song needed. They had programmed the rhythm into the Linn Drum and the band jammed over the top of it. Neither the original or the updated version are band favourites, but the song can be seen as an important step in finding the sound and direction for *Songs from the Big Chair*.

One theory is that 'Mothers Talk' samples strings from an unspecified Barry Manilow song. It's hard to decipher which one; it is possibly 'Copacabana', if true. This has been discounted by Chris Hughes, who said that the strings came from an emulator sample library.

The band's sound had expanded to being more progressive pop in this era and this track explored a more expansive tone – it's almost funk-rock in places. When talking to *Prog* magazine about the band's progressive tendencies, Orzabal said that 'Mother's Talk' was a bit of a steal from Weather Report's 'Teen Town'. The bass part at the end, in particular, was a vague tribute to WR bassist Jaco Pastorius.

The lyrical inspirations came from the Raymond Briggs book *When the Wind Blows*, a book about nuclear Armageddon, which was a concern to most in the 80s. Orzabal also appropriated an old English expression that mothers used to say to their children, 'if you pull a face, you'll stick like that when the weather changes'. The song also borrowed a line from the last line of playwright Joe Orton's 1969 farce, *What the Butler Saw* reads: 'Let us put our clothes on and face the world'.

There were three versions of the video, with the first two made for the UK and European markets in 1984. Roland and Curt were extremely unhappy with the first version and enlisted the help of director Nigel Dick to redo it. Stills from Dick's second take are featured in the *Songs from the Big Chair* liner notes, while the third was constructed around the US remix, and was released in the states in 1986. The super deluxe box sets are a good place to find the different variations of the song, including the bizarre but strangely alluring 'Beat of The Drum Mix'.

'I Believe' (Roland Orzabal)
Highest chart places: UK:23

Right in the middle of the album is the sparse and delicate song 'I Believe'. It's another crack at doing something that could have easily been on *The Hurting* and is inspired by the band's then devotion to Arthur Janov. It's not far removed from the atmosphere of 'Ideas as Opiates'.

It is another song that might have been lost as a B-side before Curt intervened. It is one of Orzabal's favourites from the album and lyrically one of the most potent songs that Tears For Fears had released at that point in their career. From being an also-ran track, it became the band's fifth single lifted from *Songs from the Big Chair*. There is a line in the lyrics that references 'casino Spanish eyes' – a line that was in the running as the title of the album at some point.

The single mix, 'I Believe (A Soulful Re-Recording)', was a remixed version of the album track. Elements were recorded live on the band's US tour, even down to the faint crowd noise at the start. The band's saxophonist Will Gregory is namechecked just before his solo.

The song was originally written for Robert Wyatt and is similar in tone and style to Elvis Costello's 'Shipbuilding'. Robert Wyatt covered Costello's song in 1982, but it failed to chart. However, on re-release the following year and it went to number 35 in the UK charts. Wyatt's second solo album, *Rock Bottom*, was one that Hughes had passed to Orzabal during the writing and recording of the album to get him to extend his musical palette. The opening track of that album 'Sea Song' was covered for the B-side of the 'I Believe' single. The liner notes of the single pay tribute to the singer: 'Dedicated to Robert Wyatt (If he's listening)' This is a reference to the song that Wyatt's former band, Soft Machine recorded, 'Dedicated to You but You Weren't Listening'.

Roland discussed 'Sea Song' and Robert Wyatt in the sleeve notes for the *Saturnine Martial & Lunatic*:

This track was the B-side to 'I Believe', which was so clearly inspired by Robert Wyatt that I thought it would be a good idea to cover one of his songs for the flip side. His voice, in my opinion, is one of the best, not something I felt I could match, but if I introduced one person to his music, then it would have been worth it.

The video is quite earnest and features a topless Orzabal singing to the camera. He is also pictured pouring his thoughts into an old reel-to-reel tape machine before it cuts to Will 'William' Gregory and his sax solo. Curt doesn't get overlooked; he pops up to play symbols! The picture sleeve for the single featured a photo Roland shot of himself in the window of a hotel room and the video was inspired by that photo. This clip was shot in an aeroplane hangar in Seattle, Washington, USA, on a break from the tour for that album.

The single has a reference to Leonard Apple, who was an alter ego of Orzabal. Apple is credited on the 'I Believe' single, where on the reverse of the picture sleeve, you can find the phrase 'Leonard Apple was a good boy at school.' 'Mr Apple' also gets a credit for the sleeve photography – the self-portrait of Roland in a hotel room. Other references to the name appear on the band's World tour of 1985 and there was also talk of 'Leonard Apple's Ungodly Hour' being a potential album title at one point.

'Broken' (Roland Orzabal)

It's another one of those Tears For Fears songs that has its origins from an earlier point in their career. As discussed earlier, the song 'We Are Broken' was originally the B-side of 'Pale Shelter (New Single Version)' in 1983. The retooled version almost feels like it was written specifically to segue into 'Head over Heels', although it developed from when the band played the songs live during earlier tours. There is a similar motif of the riff that appears again in 'Head Over Heels', making the song feel like one seamless idea. The original was synth-led, the updated version is guitar-heavy, featuring another great contribution from Neil Taylor.

'Head Over Heels/Broken' (Live) (Roland Orzabal, Curt Smith)

Highest chart places: UK:12, US:3.

The opening piano motif takes you back to summer's past and hearing the first notes can't help but make you feel nostalgic. The album version is bookended by two takes of 'Broken', while the single version strips away those songs.

'Head Over Heels' was the fourth single to be released from the album in the UK; it was one that surprisingly did not land in the top ten. Maybe at that point time, most people had heard the song and did not feel the need to buy it as a single. There was potentially overkill with the band's other successful singles that were still being played on the radio at the time of its release. It might have fared better as the choice of the first single, although, it did do well in the US.

'Head Over Heels' was written before the sessions for the *Big Chair* album and there was a feeling from within the band that it was going to be the album's big song. That's before 'Shout' and 'Everybody Wants to Rule the World' came along, of course.

It's a co-write, as Orzabal struggled to finish the song until Smith came along with a few choice lines for the lyrics. Orzabal has said that he finds it hard to write conventional love songs, so it's when the lyrics get stranger towards the end that is thought to be Orzabal's contribution. Even so, it was probably the closest that the band had got to writing a love song, even if it's not obvious – but more a hint. The singer wants to engage in small talk in the lyrics (and the video) with his love interest as an excuse to be near her 'I wanted to be with you alone/and talk about the weather'.

There is a great bassline that is reminiscent of the one from the Talking Heads' song 'Take Me to the River', while the choral vocals at the end further enhance the big arrangement – it's 'Hey Jude' moment.

We then return to 'Broken', but this time it's a live version, giving the three-part piece quite a progressive feel, while the extended guitar jams that bookend it do not do much to dispel that feeling, recreating the live feel. The live version was taken from a show at Hammersmith Odeon (now the Apollo).

Multiple versions of the song appeared in the various formats at the time. The single remix is edited at the point where Orzabal sings 'Funny how time flies' and there is a notable 12-inch extended remix of the entire 'Broken/Head Over Heels/Broken' medley called the 'Preacher Mix', which was mixed by Hughes and features a spoken word intro with Orzabal reciting the lyrics from 'I Believe' in the style of a preacher.

The video was shot in June 1985 at the Emmanuel College Library, Toronto, during the band's extensive world tour. It was directed by Nigel Dick, who had worked with the band on previous promo videos, concerts, and the band's *Scenes from the Big* Chair documentary. It's tongue in cheek compared to the other promos they had done to that point, pointing to an age when record company largesse funded cinematic MTV-friendly videos. It follows Orzabal's attempts to get the attention of a librarian while a variety of characters (played by the rest of the band) and a chimpanzee wearing a Red

Sox jersey act out in the library. Curt Smith, plays the role of the janitor, who is befriended by the chimp.

An edited version of 'Head over Heels' was featured in the 2001 film *Donnie Darko*, the same source as the famous 'Mad World' cover. Director Richard Kelly has stated the scene was written and synced with this song in mind.

'Listen' (Ian Stanley, Roland Orzabal)

The segue from the previous track gives a feeling that most of side two of the LP was almost one piece. Even though it is heavily instrumental, 'Listen' fits in with the narrative of the album. Ian Stanley devised the track on the Fairlight at his home studio and the intricacies of that system made it difficult to replicate in the studio, but Stanley painstakingly reprogrammed the machine to get the version we hear today. Perhaps it was because he was unsure of its quality until Orzabal convinced him to work on it. The collaborative element came from a second part that Orzabal had that fitted perfectly.

It's an ethereal number with an instrumental refrain that takes up the first part of the track before Curt Smith sings about Mother Russia. The lyric is nonsensical, although it's sung with conviction. The other lyrics are mostly just repeating 'cumpleaños chica, no hay que preocuparse', although many also heard 'Wrap me up a chicken tikka'. Ian Stanley had been to Kenya and knew the word for chicken, apparently!

Significantly it was the last track that the band recorded for the album. There is a Santana-like guitar line from Orzabal running throughout the song, while the title comes from someone who says 'listen' in the middle of the track – supposedly either Chris Hughes or Ian Stanley.

Again, the band's progressive elements came to the fore. Orzabal said of the song to *Prog Magazine* in 2015: 'You hear it and you think of the two words that one always associates with long, trippy music: Pink Floyd'. It's ambient, making it closer to the experiments that the band often released as B-sides.

Stand Alone Singles, B-sides, EPs and Other Contemporary Tracks

There are numerous B-sides and remixes from this period. A number have been released on deluxe editions and B-side collections, so see the entry of *Saturnine Martial & Lunatic* for the *Songs from the Big Chair* era releases not listed here.

'Everybody Wants to Run the World' (Roland Orzabal, Ian Stanley, Chris Hughes)

Highest chart places: UK: 5.

Having been approached to play the famous charity event Live Aid, the band turned down the opportunity and instead, they donated proceeds from select *Songs from the Big Chair* tour dates to the famine relief effort. The reason for not playing the gig was that they had just come off a long tour and they had lost members of their touring band.

They were also displeased that they had been announced as participants before being officially asked, but as a way of making it up to Bob Geldof, they offered a reworked version of their big hit 'Everybody Wants to Rule the World' but as 'Everybody Wants to Run the World' for the Sport Aid arm of the Live Aid charity. It's a fairly faithful version, with the obvious change of lyrics. There's a more prominent drum pattern and a new synth motif running through this version. The reworked song was released in June 1986 and several mixes can be found on the box sets of the album.

ManCrab – 'Fish for Life' (Ian Stanley, Roland Orzabal)
This is not strictly Tears For Fears release, but one that was written in the *Songs from the Big Chair* era. This was a collaboration between Orzabal and Stanley for the *Karate Kid II* movie soundtrack, featuring lead vocalist Eddie Thomas (credited as Eddie Jnr. on the single sleeve). He had previously been seen as one of the dancers in the 'Everybody Wants to Rule the World' video. The name 'Mancrab' is supposed to represent a sort of melding of humans and technology. The single was released on the United Artists label, but it did not chart on either side of the Atlantic and has been largely forgotten. It's a soulful number, not typically like Tears For Fears in tone.

The Seeds of Love

Personnel:
Curt Smith: bass, backing vocals, co-lead vocals, lead vocals
Roland Orzabal: lead vocals, backing vocals, guitars, keyboards, Fairlight programming
Oleta Adams: keyboards, co-lead vocals, acoustic piano, backing vocals
Ian Stanley: keyboards and Hammond organ
Nicky Holland: keyboards, backing vocals, piano, Kurzweil strings
Simon Clark: keyboards, synthesizer, Hammond organ
Neil Taylor: guitar, rhythm guitar
Robbie McIntosh: lead guitar, slide guitar
Randy Jacobs: guitar
Pino Palladino: bass
Phil Collins: drums
Manu Katché: drums
Chris Hughes: drums and production
Simon Phillips: drums
Luís Jardim: percussion
Carole Steele: percussion
Richard Niles: orchestral arrangement
Jon Hassell: trumpet
Peter Hope-Evans: harmonica
Kate St John: saxophone, oboe
Tessa Niles: backing vocals female vocal
Carol Kenyon: backing vocals
Maggie Ryder: backing vocals
Dolette McDonald: backing vocals
Andy Caine: backing vocals
Record label: Fontana/Mercury
Recorded: Tears For Fears and David Bascombe
Release Date: September 1989
Highest Chart Placings: UK: 1, US: 8
Run Time: 49:31

Given how long it took for the album to emerge, *The Seeds of Love* sessions probably deserve a book of their own. The album took many years, pounds, producers and musicians before it finally came together. The band always planned that their sound would evolve and they had certainly shown that development during the previous two album, but what Orzabal and Smith probably did not expect, however, was how their relationships would change in that period.

At the end of the 1985 documentary, *Scenes from the Big Chair,* Roland Orzabal outlined his hope that the band's next album would reveal a maturity in sound – something that would show a development in their musical

48

ambitions. He joked to the camera, just before the final credits rolled, that the evolution of Tears For Fears would be akin to the band revealing 'a manly, hairy chest'. This may have been a throwaway comment, but there was a desire on the part of Orzabal for the band to change. To grow up.

Coming off the back of a mammoth world tour in 1986, the band had planned to take a break before they worked on album number three. Tentatively, late 1987 was pencilled in the record label's schedule as a release date. Given their previous track record, this was not a speculative notion; they had delivered albums over a two-year cycle before and hopes for a quick release were not fanciful. The soundchecks on the band's last tour had thrown up several ideas that could be used once the sessions for the next album started in earnest. Little did Orzabal, Smith, and those associated with the band know that those sessions would take almost four years from the end of the tour before any new material would be released.

'After we recorded *Songs from the Big Chair*, all around us was a desire to recreate it [in terms of sonics and commercial success],' Roland Orzabal said to *Q Magazine* before the album's release in 1989. 'Everybody, except me and Curt felt we were on to a good thing. I couldn't see it that way; I believe to create, you have to destroy. It's painful and difficult, but it's the only way I can work'.

This is what they did. Hindsight can be a wonderful thing, but for an album that had many missteps and false starts, the starting point of *The Seeds of Love* could be traced back to a hotel bar in Kansas City. Few of their peers were getting close to the sales numbers that Tears For Fears had been achieving, yet, things were not going as they wanted for the band. The limitations of playing heavily-programmed music on their stage-side Revox machine were restrictive for musicians looking to improvise and adapt on stage.

That chance encounter with the singer Oleta Adams in Kansas was significant in many ways. In the *Classic Albums* documentary in 2020, which reflected on the legacy of *Songs from the Big Chair*, Orzabal said that meeting Oleta Adams shaped the course of the band for the next four years and beyond. Such was her influence that when the band returned to the live arena, she was installed as a touring member of the band. Adams even opened the live sets with an almost solo piano and vocal rendition of 'I Believe'.

He explained to *Q Magazine* in 1989 what he got from the experience of seeing Adams for the first time:

We played the concert, thousands of people, the vari-lights, the huge PA, and it felt vacuous. After we'd showered, we went down to the hotel bar. A dollar fifty to get in because there was a band on. There was a woman called Oleta Adams singing and playing the piano with bass and drums. It wasn't like a normal bar; there were families there, people in suits. You didn't feel you could talk; you had to listen. And it was incredible. I was in tears. She was in tears. Phenomenal atmosphere. And I thought I'm doing something wrong. I've got to go back to basics.

The story is contradicted (very slightly) by Ian Stanley, who has said that it was he that had stumbled across Adams the previous night when he had stayed up after a gig. He then alerted Orzabal of her act, and various members of the band turned up to watch her on the night that Orzabal details. Whatever the timeline of events, there is no denying the significance of the encounter with Adams.

After the gruelling promotional campaign and extensive tours of 1985 and 1986, the following year was seen as a time to take stock and rest up before the band started work on the new album. Restless to get started, Orzabal broke ranks and began to develop songs and ideas for the next album. At that time, he and his wife had moved to London, while Curt Smith was still living in Bath. This made it difficult for the pair to connect in the initial stages, so Smith's involvement was limited early on. That would set the scene for what followed.

Things seemed to be going well. Ideas were coming together and there were even a few suggestions as to what the album would be called. *Raoul and the Kings of Spain* (which was later used as the title for Tears For Fears' fifth album) was suggested. *Zen and the Kings of Bohemia* named after a pub in North London, was another idea. *Sowing the Seeds of Love* was also in the running, which would be abbreviated for the eventual album title.

Orzabal had always been seen as the band's principal songwriter, but initially, he worked with Nicky Holland an ex-member of a band called The Ravishing Beauties and the musical director for The Funboy Three. She had also been playing keyboards with the band on the *Songs from the Big Chair* tour. These sessions proved productive for the pair and would form the initial batch of songs that they would share between the band and associates, having previously collaborated on the Robert Wyatt cover 'Sea Song'. She said how she started collaborating with Orzabal came about in the sheet music book of the album in 1990:

> Although the Wyatt song was obviously a cover and thus involved no composition or writing, we did our arrangement of it. The whole thing came together in a day and we both loved the way it turned out. The song was an indication that Roland and I could work together. With hindsight, it was something of a turning point.

The development of the new album was stepped up a notch late in 1986 when Orzabal and Smith began working with producers Clive Langer and Alan Winstanley. The pair had success producing Madness, The Teardrop Explodes, and Elvis Costello in the past, and it was hoped that they could help bring that to the development of a more organic sound for Tears For Fears. But there was a quick realisation that the Langer and Winstanley experiment was a mistake. It is interesting to hear the fruits of these early sessions on *disc four, the wind – demos, diversions & jams,* of the super deluxe edition of the album. It contains a number of the songs from these sessions, many of which would appear on the final version of the album but in a markedly different form.

In early 1987, they looked again to their long-time collaborator Chris Hughes to get them back on course. He had always been seen as something of a talisman for the band. Hughes again stepped in to help shape the next phase following the aborted Langer and Winstanley sessions. Given label concerns, his presence was seen as a reassuring one for all concerned.

Hughes, the producer of the previous albums and Ian Stanley, co-producer and sometimes songwriter, were sent demos of the work in progress. The initial songs and ideas were not well-received by the pair. The songs also did not find favour with the other main players associated with the band, notably David Bates, who was unsure of the direction the band were talking. Having been involved in numerous disagreements with Orzabal and Smith in the latter stages of 1985 about musical direction, tensions were already present in their relationship, so the new songs exacerbated these issues, with Bates firmly ensconced in the camp that would have preferred a *Songs from the Big Chair* Mark II; something that would reap similar sales figures for the record label.

The one lone voice championing the songs at the time was Curt Smith, as he explained to *Q Magazine* in 1989

There are times when everybody else is telling Roland that what he's doing is wrong. That's when I'll be there saying. It's the right stuff, don't ever lose confidence in it. It was like that with this new material. I loved it from the word go. It was everything I wanted us to be.

Despite some of his initial misgivings of the first set of songs he had heard, Hughes was impressed by some of the newer material. Orzabal was convinced that Hughes was finally on board with the way he wanted to shape the album when he played him one of the songs that he had co-written with Nicky Holland but had never made it on to the final album, telling Q:

I sang Chris a song called *Rhythm of Life* with piano and drum machine accompaniment and he said, That's incredible! You should record it like that, keep it simple; that's dead right. I thought He was getting the message! So, we decided to go ahead.

The initial sessions took place at Roland's London house, as well as Trevor Horn's Sarm Studios, and George Martin's Air Studios in September, with Stanley on keyboards, Hughes on drums and Neil Taylor on guitar. They then switched to Virgin's Townhouse Studios and Peter Gabriel's Real World at Box, near Bath. The results of these sessions proved to be unsuccessful. The band had lapsed into familiar routines.

Orzabal said about the process to *Q Magazine:*

On *Rhythm of Life,* which we'd meant to keep simple, it transpired that we took about six weeks pissing about with a drum machine,' Something with which bandmate Curt Smith concurred. 'Ah, those days sitting around the Fairlight! Such an exciting time it was. We'd slipped back into a comfortable relationship. We got on well with Chris 99 per cent of the time, and we still do. That was the trouble.

After eleven months of working with Hughes, the band and producer went their separate ways. The results of the sessions were seen as 'sterile'. An argument between Hughes and Orzabal put an end to this phase in the recording process over the trivial matter of how the guitar was sounding on a recording, but this left the band no further down the line in terms of getting the album ready for release. The record label was getting concerned at this point, given the lack of progress.

Ian Stanley felt that he should have been recognised as more of an equal partner in the band, given his previous contributions. Not because he wanted it from the point of view of being a pop star, but in terms of recognition. However, he also wanted to spread his wings and produce other people, as well as do film scores. Stanley had been a big presence on the previous albums but here was only really present on the Hammond organ for the big leadoff single. Arguably, the move from synths to Oleta Adam's piano meant that Stanley's contributions would have been less anyway. He also moved on.

With the new album struggling to come together, the band needed something that would give them impetus. The failed experiments with new producers had been a chastening experience for the band. They looked back again into their recent history to a moment that had a profound effect on them as musicians. Going nowhere fast, they decided to go and seek out Oleta Adams. In December 1987, they went back to Kansas, where they found the singer playing solo in a smaller bar. They listened to her perform and were again convinced that she should help shape the next phase of the band.

The logical step was for the band to produce the record themselves, particularly as Orzabal had deemed himself 'unproducible' at the time. However, this was something that needed to be signed off by the label, Phonogram and David Bates was reluctant to agree. Bates said to *Q Magazine* 1989.

He [Orzabal] said, 'This is going to sound mad and not make you happy, but … we want to produce the album ourselves. Give us a chance. I think I know how it should be. I write the songs; I play them, I've got a vision.' Here we were a year in, and everything was scrapped. There'd been no previous indication that Roland was a producer. He knew I'd be nervous, but he said. 'Just tell me as soon as you don't like something'. I bit my tongue and said, 'OK, let's see what happens.'

Given the experience so far, this was the only way forward for the band. Orzabal admitted that it was his singular vision for the next phase of the band that was getting in the way of making progress with other producers.

So, almost two years down the line, the band were no closer to the record being completed. After two albums created mostly on Fairlight synthesizers, the duo got their wish for a more organic-sounding record. The next phase of the project would see Oleta Adams, drummer Manu Katche, Neil Taylor, bassist Pino Palladino, percussionist Carole Steele and keyboardist Simon Clark assemble for the first of the sessions produced by Orzabal in London in February 1988. Smith and Orzabal set up the band to play while they orchestrated things from the comfort of the control booth. There were numerous takes from these sessions. There were meticulously dissected and edited and rearranged to find the perfect versions of the songs.

The works of the group of musicians who appeared at these original sessions only made it onto three of the album's songs, with Orzabal and Smith performing much of the remaining five tracks.

One of the ironies of the recording process is that the band went for a more organic approach, but the album was still heavily indebted to the use of the technology of the age, specifically the Fairlight. The epic first single from the album, 'Sowing the Seeds of Love', was something that was formed through this process, while 'Badman's Song' was another patchwork quilt of a song.

By July 1988, the record label was beginning to get twitchy that the new album had not been finished. This exacerbated the tensions between the band and Dave Bates. Orzabal's view was that Bates was 'highly confrontational' and Bates thought that Orzabal was 'a moody bugger'. A new deadline of March 1989 was agreed upon – over four years since the release of *Songs from the Big Chair*. The sessions rumbled on for another year. The March deadline passed without any sign of the album being completed. The final day came a few months later, on 15 July 1989.

But despite the misgivings from the label across the many months, they were happy with the finished results. Dave Bates said to *Q Magazine* in 1989, 'I was shitting myself before these playbacks, I was on sleeping tablets — this is it, are they going to like it? But they all went nuts. And 'Badman's Song', which was such an appalling mess all that time ago, is one of the best tracks on it'.

The album was finally released in September 1989, going to number one in the UK and spent 30 weeks on the chart, which may have vindicated the time spent putting the album together. The estimated £1 million it cost to record the album was recouped over time. According to Phil Sutcliffe in *Q Magazine*, even this figure led to disagreements between the band.

[It's £1 million] If you accept Curt Smith's view, or £4-500,000 if you go along with Dave Bates — the A&R man reckons Smith came up with an exaggerated figure by counting studio equipment that Tears For Fears have bought for use on the album but which stands to them as a capital asset rather than a loss.

The contrast between the cover for this album and those before that preceded it is remarkable. Out went the stark monochrome images of the pair for *Songs*

from the Big Chair, and in came the bold, colourful 60s-influenced cover
of *The Seeds of Love*. Out with the psychological, in with the spiritual and
astrological. Some of the lyrical themes are symbolised on the front cover.
There are the yin and the yang symbol and the sunflower is front and centre
above the pair dressed in colourful suits. Orzabal is wearing a blue suit and
holding an umbrella with a fish ornament adorning it, while Smith is dressed
resplendently in his gold suit, holding up a staff with a sun attached. The
astrological themes reflect the interests and influences of Orzabal, symbolising
the water and fire elements associated with Cancer (Smith's zodiac sign) and
Leo (Orzabal's zodiac sign), respectively. There's also a little bit of Miró; a style
rejected for the last album. This time it is represented in some of the figures
that make up the rest of the cover. The is as bold as the songs on the album.

Super Deluxe Edition Box Set
The band's third deluxe edition release follows a similar template to the
previous box sets. Disc one contains the original album. The second disc is
called *The Sun,* which is made up of singles from different territories and
B-sides, plus mixes of 'Johnny Panic and The Bible of Dreams'. Disc three
is *The Moon* which has radio edits and early mixes. Disc four, *The Wind* has
demos, diversions and jams. These are worth listening to hear the songs in
their primitive states, taken from the Townhouse jams and the Langer and
Winstanley sessions. The final disc is a DVD called *The Rain,* featuring the
various *The Seeds of Love* mixes, including the Steven Wilson 5.1 Mix, The
Original Album Mix (Bob Ludwig 1989 mastering) and 2015 new remaster
(by Andrew Walter at Abbey Road). The box set as ever comes with a detailed
booklet and a reproduction of *The Seeds of Love* tour programme.

'Woman in Chains' (Roland Orzabal)
Highest chart places: UK: 26, US: 36.
From the opening bars of the album's first track, it is clear that the band's
sound had matured in the time since the release of *Songs from the Big Chair.*
This is the tune that introduces the vocal talents of Oleta Adams, who on this
track alone justifies the decision to integrate her into the band.
   In a band that has always mined their personal experiences for songs, the
sophisticated 'Women in Chains' is no different. The song is a feminist anthem
written about Orzabal's mother's experience of domestic violence. It is also
a song that is reflective of a patriarchal society. It was a song that saw them
criticised by their peers at the time, who suggested that they were too young
to write about this type of subject. Orzabal spoke to the *Washington Post* at the
time of release: 'I'm singing about the oppression of women around the world,
but I'm also singing about the repression of the female anima within myself. In
the end, when I sing, 'Free her', I'm also saying, 'Free me''.
   The brief was to make the song sound like 'Avalon' by Roxy Music. In keeping
with the nature of the way that the album was recorded, 'Women in Chains' has

several notable contributions. Somewhere in the mix is drummer Phil Collins, who was asked to guest on the track. His 'bit' can be found just before the key change, although there are other drummers on the song and their parts have been woven together. The band wanted that trademark 'In the Air Tonight' fill from Collins, which he did not deliver, but something just as appropriate. The band had set aside a few days for him to do his recording, but Curt Smith remembered Collins's response was in the album's SDE liner notes: 'Days? For one track? I'll come in at lunch and be home for tea.' Orzabal and Smith could only watch in awe as, in contrast to much more difficult sessions during the creation of the album, he nailed his part with ease.

It is a sumptuously produced number with a beautifully haunting flute motif that runs through the song, while Neil Taylor's guitar arpeggio is beautiful. There's a great bassline that rumbles throughout the song, though parts of it are sampled. Orzabal delivers the most soulful vocal of his career to date, while Oleta Adam's said at the time of the release of her part, that it 'contains some of the best singing that I have ever done. Talk about perfectionism. Roland's attention to detail is amazing, running as far as getting just the right emphasis on the letter 'p' in the word 'hope''.

There's a lot of heart and soul in the song. The lyrics and performances come deep from within, even though the recording and rewriting of this song went up to the wire in the release schedule.

It has twice been released as a single, but it did not find the upper reaches of the charts either time. It was the second single released off the album and reached 26 in the UK in 1989. The second time it was released was in 1992 as part of the campaign for the band's greatest hits package, credited to Tears For Fears, featuring Oleta Adams. It remains a staple of the band's live set and is a firm fan favourite.

The video Is a moody black and white affair that has the narrative of the boxer and the strip club dancer. This is a call back to the reference to the 'great white hope' in the song. This was originally a nickname given to James Jeffries, a white boxer defeated by the first black heavyweight champion, Jack Johnson, in 1910. In the 'Woman in Chains' video, the protagonist's husband is a boxer and also a domestic abuser – a metaphorical reference to the domestic abuse that Orzabal witnessed as a child.

'Badman's Song' (Roland Orzabal, Nicky Holland)

The extended jazz workout was one of the first songs that would materialise during the protracted recording sessions for *The Seeds of Love*. It was something that was developed by Orzabal and Nicky Holland during soundchecks on the *Songs from the Big Chair* world tour. While it came together initially, he sang the 'in my head' line and then Holland responded with a few chords on the piano. The collaborative partnership saw Holland complementing Orzabal's guitar-oriented style with her rather more classical influences. During the initial stages of the song coming together, it wasn't yet a duet; that would come later. Indeed, it was not even a gospel-tinged song which would begin to emerge when Oleta Adams became involved.

The recording of 'Badman's Song' is symbolic of how protracted recording sessions were. Co-writer Nicky Holland has said that the band went through many arrangements before they settled on the jazz/gospel-inspired version, whereas earlier arrangements have been inspired by bands such as Little Feat and Steely Dan. Dave Bascombe, the album's co-producer, has also commented on the song's difference from the original demo. This demo, recorded with producers Clive Langer and Alan Winstanley, can be found on the fourth disc of the super deluxe edition. You can also find 'Medley/Reprise/Townhouse Live Jam Sessions,' and 'Townhouse Live Jam Sessions', which help plot the evolution of the song.

Given its length, the track was never in the running to be a single, but it appeared as an extra track on the 'Women in Chains' re-release in 1992. There is a live version that clocks in at well over 11 minutes on *Knebworth: The Album 1990,* taken from a live recording from a gig that raised money for the Nordoff-Robbins music charity.

The evolution of the song also marked the first sign of the tensions between Orzabal and Smith and Ian Stanley, while the band's management and record label were not convinced with these early versions either. 'Badman's Song' in its completed form weighs in at just under nine minutes and is one of five compositions on the album that were co-written between Orzabal and Holland.

The lyrical inspirations come from an overheard conversation. On the sleeve notes, there is a reference to 'the boys back in 628 – all is forgiven'. In the song itself, there is a line that references the boys '...where an ear to the wall was a twist of fate'. This relates to an overheard conversation back at the hotel after a show at Denver Red Rocks on the band's previous world tour. There was a party featuring members of the band's crew going on in the room next to Orzabal; they were making noise that was keeping him up. He put his ear to the wall and he heard them criticising him and the band. Orzabal finished the chorus the next day. He was even complimented on the lyrics by one of the offending crew members at that evening's soundcheck when he gave the song a quick run-through.

It's a song about guilt and remorse. It contains a great deal of catholic imagery, with numerous biblical references, with 'faith moving mountains', and 'fire cleansing souls'. 'Sticks and Stones may break my bones, but at least the seeds of love will be sown' is one of the telling couplets in the song.

'Sowing the Seeds of Love' (Roland Orzabal, Curt Smith)
Highest chart places: UK:5, US:2
When the band re-emerged in September 1989, the album was proceeded by the Beatlesque lead single 'Sowing the Seeds of Love'. Orzabal has not hidden the fact that the song is a 'minor scale' version of The Beatles' classic 'I am The Walrus'. He laboriously used the Fairlight, to put the song together, which

seemingly took forever. Although, Dave Bascombe believes that it might have been The Rutles 'Piggy in the Middle' that was the main inspiration, a pastiche of 'I Am the Walrus' from Eric Idle and Neil Innes' parody of The Fab Four that they used instead to track the rhythm. He told Paul Sinclair in 2019 that:

> To get the template for the tempo, we didn't use 'I Am the Walrus'; we used 'Piggy In The Middle' by The Rutles. I remember borrowing the album from my manager; I don't think I ever gave it back.

The rhythm track on the original demo, however, had a more hop-hip influence, giving it a Prince-like tone.

This epic Beatles/Summer of Love-inspired comeback single in 1989 marked a distinct change in approach for the band. The vocals are very distorted, evoking singers like Dylan, Lennon and Bowie. Chris Hughes on drums does a great impression of Ringo's trademark fills. In typical fashion, the live drums were then sequenced digitally.

Other parts were recorded that did not make it into the finished version. The song is epic in its finished form, clocking in just under seven minutes in length. It had the potential to be even longer, with as many as six middle-eights being written for the song but not used. Given the number of extra sections it could have had, comparisons with The Beach Boys 'Good Vibrations' are not far off the mark, particularly as both songs try to get across a sunny vibe.

Curt Smith often feels absent on the album. Most of the bass parts, in particular, were performed by session musicians or samples. He may have been side-lined by his colleague's single-minded approach to the album, but at least he did play a big part in the writing of the album's biggest tune and it's the only song in which he gets a co-write. Initially, the chorus contained only the chords and the line 'anything is possible when you're sowing the seeds of love'. However, Curt came in and started singing the hooky line that is part of the chorus. For Orzabal, that was a missing piece of the puzzle.

Ian Stanley was still around when the first versions of the song were recorded. He provides the lush Hammond organ solo that appears midway through the song and the version that is on the record is from a first take.

Lyrically the song saw the shift from the personal to the political for Orzabal. It was written in the final years of the Thatcher government and it was a time when he became more politically aware. He had been reading books on Marxism and these ideas spilt into the lyrics. 'Politician granny with your high ideals' is one such line that showed this awareness of the times. The song was also inspired by a chance programme on BBC Radio 4, which featured a discussion about a historian who was putting together a collection of English folk tunes that had been passed down generations by word of mouth. One of the songs was by Mr England and was called 'The Seeds of Love'. Hence the line 'Mr England, sowing the seeds of love.' This Inspired a lyric and the overall theme of the song, which also inspired the imagery of the album cover.

Roland told *Melody Maker* at the time about some graffiti which helped inspire a lyric and the album's imagery:

'I love a sunflower' is a piece of graffiti on a wall near my home. I see it every day. I didn't know what to sing on a guide vocal for the track, so I sang that instead of 'dada dada dada'. Then all of a sudden, 'Sowing the Seeds' is just about to come out and the Ecology Party does well in the Euro-elections and their emblem is the sunflower. I didn't know that; it all seems to be fitting in now. These things are synchronous.

The song also references MC5's 'Kick Out the Jams' with the line 'Kick out the style! Bring back the jam!', also an oblique reference to Orzabal's preference for Paul Weller's previous band The Jam over his more recent outfit The Style Council. A debate much discussed at the time in the UK.

Curt Smith has said that the song is the most complete piece of work that the band have ever created – far more 'musical' than anything that they had recorded to this point, while Orzabal's love of all things astrological is strongly represented; the sun and the moon in *The Seeds of Love* artwork represent himself and Smith, respectively, as the sun is the ruler of Leo (Orzabal's zodiac sign, and the moon is the ruler of Cancer (Smith's zodiac sign). These are the visuals that can be seen on the artwork and the videos for the release. Lyrically the sun, moon, wind, and rain motifs appear throughout the album, and as we have seen, these elements are even used as the titles for extra discs on the super deluxe box set of the album

For an eight-track album, there are some hefty cuts. The single release of 'The Seeds of Love' is 5:46 long while the album version is 6:19. The longest version that they released can be found on the box set's third disc and which weighs in at 7:19 called the 'Alternate Mix'.

In the UK, the single went in at number five and spent nine weeks on the charts. It missed out on a US number one because of record company politics at the band's label over there. It was ahead on sales but lost out on airplay to Janet Jackson's 'Miss You Much'. Orzabal said to *SDE* 'Once 'Sowing the Seeds of Love' 'only' got to number two [in the US], it gave the American record company an excuse to take their foot off the gas'. The suggestion is that the US label thought the album lacked further potential hits.

The video is an epic in itself. It embraces the pastoral and the sunshine vibes of the lyrics, and the mix of live footage and animation is striking with plenty of pastoral imagery. The visual themes of the album cover are also replicated. The song still stands up brilliantly today.

'Advice for the Young at Heart' (Roland Orzabal, Nicky Holland)
Highest chart places: UK: 36, US: 89
This was the third single and the only full lead vocal from Smith on the album. Originally Orzabal tried a vocal, but it didn't work. Listening to the

demo (disc four on *The Seeds of Love* Super Deluxe Edition), it's not a bad take on the song.

It's a pleasant number that has a summery vibe to it – the perfect companion piece to the lead single. The band did not score that well with singles for this album with 'Sowing' overshadowing everything else that followed, although 'Advice' feels like an obvious single given that it is one of the shorter songs. Lyrically the song is about growing older and there are also nods to past tracks, especially via the 'working hour is over' line.

Orzabal outlined the background to the song in the sheet music book of the album: 'The song expresses a desire to grow up and get things together – to let go of the past. I think it's just an awareness of getting older; that's what it stems from. And also, an awareness that certain aspects of you aren't getting older'.

It's another of the Orzabal and Holland co-writes and was written back in 1986. Indeed, the structure of the song did not change that much from the early demos, although eventually, Orzabal added the extended guitar break in the middle – something Holland did not like, preferring the song in its earlier form. The original demo also contains the musical motif that appears in the song 'Standing on the Corner of the Third World', which suggests the original idea was for the song to act as a segue in a similar vein to 'Broken/Head Over Heels/Broken (Live)' which appears on *Songs from the Big Chair*.

The video features the touring band of the time playing in what looks like a Spanish hacienda, mixed with a wedding story.

'Standing on the Corner of the Third World' (Roland Orzabal)

There is a definite tonal shift in the second half of the album. The flipside is very introspective. Only 'Year of the Knife' breaks the mellow jazzy vibe. This is another song that mines the personal and the political. It was also a song that came out of Orzabal's experiences of therapy.

It takes on globalisation and colonialism. The lyrics reflect on the relative comfort and safety that people in the west have, while other things that are going on in the world get ignored. The line 'compassion is the fashion' may have been a subtle dig at the big charity events that took place in the era. Orzabal said in the album's book of sheet music:

It is about conflict and contrasts between a feeling of security and the threats of life's darker areas. It is about having one foot in the womb, happy in the sense of cosy containment, and one foot in the backroads and basements of our lives.

Yazz, who had a hit in the UK with 'The Only Way is Up' was one of the backing singers, although she was not credited on the sleeve notes. There's an evocative piano part played by Oleta Adams and a rumbling bassline by Pino Palladino. Some elements of the song sound reminiscent of Peter

Gabriel's 1980s output. It embraces the same lush orchestration that had been employed to good effect on the 1986 *So* album, while Gabriel's drummer, Manu Katché plays on the song. The trumpeter Jon Hassell also features. It's yet another song that has a stellar cast of session musicians credited in the sleeve notes.

On *The Seeds of Love* box set, the 'Townhouse Jam' version of the song is 9:12, and while the bulk of the song is similar to the version that was released, this lengthier version includes an extended jam as the outro. Oleta Adams' piano playing can be heard in greater detail in the outro of that version.

'Swords and Knives' (Roland Orzabal, Nicky Holland)

It's another song that was developed during soundchecks on the band's last tour and was inspired by Deborah Spungen's book, *I Don't want to Live This Life*, that Nicky Holland had read. The author was the mother of Nancy Spungen, who was murdered by her boyfriend Sid Vicious, the Sex Pistols bassist. Holland passed the book on to Orzabal, who then wrote the lyrics to the song.

It was the first demo that was completed for the new album and it began life in a different form. Holland explained the inspiration for the music in the accompanying sheet music book. 'The song began as a piano piece, reminiscent of Eric Satie and Claud Debussy. Roland thought that it sounded like a film theme, a leitmotif that recurs throughout the picture in different shapes and sizes'. Chris Hughes had suggested that the middle section should be stretched out, before the return of the initial theme. That section is missing from the original demo that appears on the album's deluxe box set, although the piano motif is still present.

Lyrically it returns to themes that the band had covered on *The Hurting*, in particular, songs like 'Suffer the Children'. 'Swords and Knives' talks about an 'A waking world of innocence. So, grave those first-born cries. When life begins with needles and pins. It ends with swords and knives'. 'Swords and knives' is a reference to Deborah Spungen's book.

The band offered the demo of the song to Alex Cox for his film *Sid and Nancy*. Cox rejected it deeming that the song 'wasn't punk enough'. With a run time of 6:13, it is understandable why that is the case. The song is more akin to something more progressive than punk. A form that was the antithesis of all that punk was supposed to have stood for. Although, In the fullness of time, it was clear that the notable punk rockers, like John Lydon, hadn't thrown own out their prog rock records as they said they had.

The song is an expansive piece, with the 'stretched out' middle section home to a great guitar part (possibly from Roland Orzabal) that leads us back to the vocal elements towards the end. There are notable performances from Tessa Niles, who provides 'backing' vocals, but in the mix she acts as a co-lead vocalist for much of the song. Kate St John provides both saxophone and oboe, which adds to the atmospheric nature of the song.

'Year of the Knife' (Roland Orzabal, Nicky Holland)

There are many versions of this song on the super deluxe box sets and it seems that this number was in the running to be selected as a single. In its album version, it's quite a sprawling and epic number, while the single edit cuts out most of this and offers up a leaner version. Initially in the running to be the opening number, it's the most aggressive song on *The Seeds of Love*, and quite possibly the most assertive song that the band had ever released. Indeed, there are four guitarists battling it out in the mix, Orzabal, Neil Taylor, Robbie McIntosh, and Randy Jacob, of Was (Not) Was, with McIntosh taking the lead parts.

It's an out-and-out rocker, and in breaking the flow of intense songs, It serves the same function that 'Broken' did on *Songs from the Big Chair* – a buffer between the mid-tempo songs and ballads. It even cribs 'Broken' with its live crowd noise at the start, taken from a recording of a 1985 concert in Dallas.

A *Record Collector* review in December 1989 suggested that 'Year of the Knife' was Tears For Fears taking on U2 in the emotional rock stakes.

'Famous Last Words' (Roland Orzabal, Nicky Holland)

Highest chart places: UK: 83

The song is about the acceptance of death and overcoming the taboos surrounding the subject. The original title was going to be 'The 17-Year Locust', while the eventual one was inspired by Elvis Costello's album *Goodbye Cruel World*. To Orzabal, 'Famous Last Words' had a 'vague echo' of that.

It was also inspired by the book *The Fate of The Earth* by Jonathan Schell. It's about what two lovers would do in the last hours after a nuclear attack, with the lyrics talking about their 'real-life situations', 'sitting by candlelight' and 'listening to the band that made them cry'.

There was a suggestion at the time that it may well have been the band's last album and this is a slow and gentle fade. This solemn ballad has an ethereal quality to it that fits in with the mature sound that is typified by *The Seeds of Love*. There are some beautiful piano parts throughout the song; another great Nicky Holland contribution. There is also a beautifully evocative Orzabal vocal, albeit one that he was reluctant to sing, although Chris Hughes thinks the vocals may be too quiet.

Tom Waits was asked to sing the final verse of 'Famous Last Words' – but according to SDE he impolitely declined. 'Tears For Fears? They can fuck off', was his reaction to the invitation.

There is a snippet of spoken word at the beginning of the track: 'Let's take five minutes'. It's a bit of studio chat that somehow made it onto the tape. This is a throw-away remark about the laboured process that it took to record the album. It was released as the final UK single from the album, but it stalled at number 83.

Stand Alone Singles, B-sides, EPs and Other Contemporary Tracks

There are numerous B-sides and remixes from this period, a number have been released on deluxe editions and B-side collections; see the entry of *Saturnine Martial & Lunatic* for songs from *The Seeds of Love* era not listed here.

The box set is worth checking out for numerous versions of these songs. There are unreleased demos, alternate versions, the Townhouse jams, the Langer and Winstanley versions, plus a DVD of the Steve Wilson 5.1 mix. Wilson – solo artist, producer and ex-Porcupine Tree frontman – refused to touch the stereo mix of the album, saying that it was already 'pretty much perfect,' but he did make a 5.1 channel surround sound mix of it. It is one of the jewels of the 2020 box set.

'Music for Tables' (Roland Orzabal)

A B-side that did not make it to the *Saturnine Martial & Lunatic* album. It was originally one of the B-sides, extra tracks on the 'Advice for the Young' at Heart single. It's a jazzy piano and sax-led number. It is an extra in every sense of the word. It's filler, but quite a pretty background filler. It can also be found on *The Seeds of Love* deluxe editions.

'Rhythm of Life' (Roland Orzabal, Nicky Holland)

It was one of the first pieces that the band wrote for the *Seeds of Love* and it was so early in the sessions that Chris Hughes was still involved in the recording process. When Orzabal handed over a sparse version of the song, Hughes liked it but sought to make it more expansive, bringing about the moment when Orzabal thought that they might not have been on the same page in what they wanted.

Listed on the boxset as 'Rhythm of Love', 'Rhythm of Life' would eventually end up on the Oleta Adams solo album *Circle of One* produced by Orzabal with Dave Bascombe. It was left off the album as it was felt to be more of a soul song than a Tears For Fears number. As a result, it was a natural fit for Oleta's album.

Elemental

Personnel:
Roland Orzabal: producer, vocals, instruments
Alan Griffiths: producer, instruments
Tim Palmer: producer, instruments
Guy Pratt: additional bass guitar
John Baker: backing vocals
Julian Orzabal: backing vocals
Bob Ludwig: mastering
Mark O'Donoughue: engineer, Wurlitzer
Record label: Phonogram/Mercury
Recorded: Roland Orzabal, Alan Griffiths, and Tim Palmer
Release Date: 7th June 1993
Highest Chart Placings: UK: 5, US: 45
Run Time: 46:51

In the four years after the release of *The Seeds of Love,* Tears For Fears toured, lost a member, released a greatest hits collection, and returned with a new album. The split was an acrimonious divorce between Smith and Orzabal. The drawn-out period of recording the last album had exacerbated the divisions in the band, with Smith's contributions reduced.

Chris Hughes talking in the liner notes for *The Seeds of Love* deluxe edition box set, said: 'You can look at *Seeds of Love* as the beginning of solo Roland. You know, how much Curt got involved, how much he sang, was diminishing. You can plot that curve'.

Smith, whose songwriting contributions on the first two albums had been limited, chipped in with a co-writing credit on 'Sowing the Seeds of Love', but in truth, his contribution had become lessened throughout the album as the dynamics of the band had shifted.

He was also experiencing some personal issues as his first marriage was failing. During the subsequent tour, Curt Smith announced to Orzabal that he had had enough and would be leaving after they had finished the live dates. He had met his future wife, Frances in 1988 and was travelling back and forth to New York. In the liner notes for *The Seeds of Love* super deluxe edition box set, he explained his reasons:

When we'd done the album, I knew I was leaving. I told Roland. In retrospect, probably not a good idea to decide before the tour, I should have left it to the end. It was a combination of things. I just wasn't enjoying it anymore.

This made the tensions between the pair all the more pronounced. To get through the tour there were two camps in existence. Orzabal says in the sleeve notes of the deluxe edition of the album:

Curt and a few others used to wear T-shirts with 'B.B.C' written on them, 'Bad Boys' Club', and then [on the other side] you had me, Oleta, and her boyfriend at that time – very different factions.

David Bates said that another catalyst for the split was when he had to break it to Roland and Curt that their manager Paul King had been embezzling them. For Bates, it was probably the worst disagreement that he had seen the pair have. He felt that their relationship fell away from that point onwards. Roland says in the sleeve notes of the deluxe edition of the album:

The straw that broke the camel's back was the fact that we had a manager, Paul King, who went bankrupt, but before he went bankrupt, took the profits from our South American tour and ran off with them. I think Curt was friendly with Paul and I wasn't. Curt didn't see it as wrongdoing and I did. Our lawyer saw it as wrongdoing, so Curt got a different lawyer! But that's when we had the big falling out, we had the meeting in the concert marquee in LA. and we did Knebworth – that was our final show. I didn't even bother to say goodbye to Curt.

Orzabal reflected before the release of *The Tipping Point,* the band's seventh album that the partners should never have split as there was still much that they could have done. He told *Record Collector* in 2014 that: 'It would have been easy to get Curt in on Elemental and sing the songs. Those songs were built for him. I hadn't stopped writing for a voice. I was just singing them myself'.

With all the negatives that had happened, Orzabal could point to some positives in that period. He became a father during the time that he was recording *Elemental.* The change in his domestic arrangements saw the album being recorded primarily in Orzabal's home studio, Neptune's Kitchen. It was a space where he could 'head back to my roots and change nappies at the same time as recording'.

Elemental was a telling title of the new album in the post-Curt period. Given the trials and tribulations of the recording of the *Seeds of Love,* the fourth album was a reset. The musical landscape was in the process of change. Bands that had emerged in the last decade were evolving or fading away into irrelevance. For instance, bands like U2 changed their sound from something that had run its course in the late 1980s to one embracing a more alternative sensibility, as well as incorporating dance beats.

It was a period when bands from the US were in ascendancy. Nirvana's success opened the door to other Grunge bands like Pearl Jam. In the UK, the charts were full of relatively anonymous artists writing music that was primarily for the clubs, and acts like Altern8. Several alternative British bands were sowing the seeds for Britpop's emergence, and bands like Blur, Suede and Radiohead all released albums in the same year that *Elemental* was released.

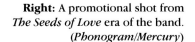

Left: We are the Mods! The regimented look of Roland and Curt's first band Graduate. (*Precision*)

Right: A promotional shot from *The Seeds of Love* era of the band. (*Phonogram/Mercury*)

Above: The pair on *BBC Breakfast* in 2022. The interview was recorded on the day the Russia/Ukraine conflict started but was broadcast at a later date. (*BBC*)

Tears For Fears
the hurting

Left: *The Hurting's* minimalist front cover was rejected in some territories for being too sombre. *(Phonogram/Mercury)*

Right: Curt looks out the window pensively while Roland limbers up to do 'that dance' in the 'Mad World' video. *(Phonogram/Mercury)*

Left: One of the band's earliest appearances on BBC's *Top of the Pops* celebrating their first top ten hit 'Mad World'. *(BBC)*

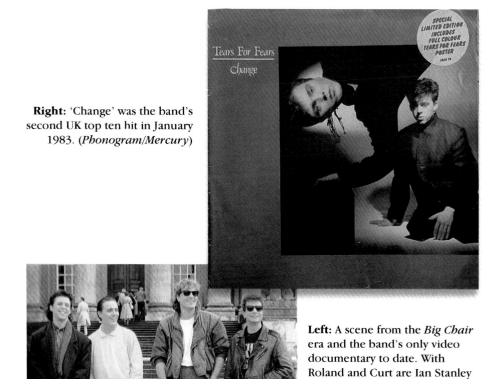

Right: 'Change' was the band's second UK top ten hit in January 1983. (*Phonogram/Mercury*)

Left: A scene from the *Big Chair* era and the band's only video documentary to date. With Roland and Curt are Ian Stanley and Manny Elias. (*Phonogram/Mercury*)

Right: The cover of 'The Way You Are', an experimental single from 1983. It represented a line under the first phase and the start of the next one. (*Phonogram/Mercury*)

Left: Another experiment – the first version of 'Mother's Talk' – helped the band find the direction for their next album. (*Phonogram/Mercury*)

Right: Another single, another appearance on *Top of the Pops*. This time for 'Mother's Talk'. (BBC)

Left: The distinctive, era-defining cover of *Songs from the Big Chair*. (*Phonogram/Mercury*)

Right: Roland letting it all out on *Top of the Pops*. *(BBC)*

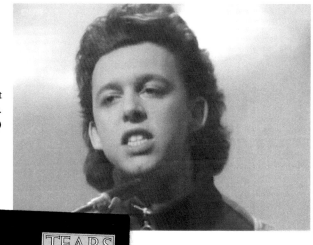

Left: One of the biggest-selling releases of the 1980s and it's still doing well on streaming platforms today, 'Everybody Wants to Rule the World'. *(Phonogram/Mercury)*

Right: The cover for the 12-inch single of 'Head Over Heels/ Broken'. *(Phonogram/Mercury)*

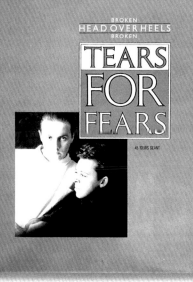

Left: The ornate cover of *The Seeds of Love* marked the band's first album release in over four years, in 1989. (*Fontana/Mercury*)

Right: Curt Smith's starring role in the 'Sowing the Seeds of Love' video. (*Fontana/Mercury*)

Left: The third single from *The Seeds of Love* and the only one that had Curt Smith as the lead vocalist during this period. (*Fontana/Mercury*)

Right: The cover for the first release of 'Women in Chains'. It would later be released again as a single with a modified image and the extra credit 'featuring Oleta Adams'. (*Fontana/Mercury*)

Left: Oleta Adams was an inspiration for the change in course during the difficult sessions that led up to the release of *The Seeds of Love*. (*Fontana/Mercury*)

Right: *Going to California*. A scene from the band's long-form video released in 1990. It captured the band during *The Seeds of Love* tour. (*Fontana/Mercury*)

TEARS FOR FEARS
Laid So Low (Tears Roll Down)

Left: The first single of the Roland' solo' era of Tears For Fears. It was a new track on the *Tears Roll Down (Greatest Hits 82–92)* compilation. (*Fontana/Mercury*)

TEARS FOR FEARS ❦ ELEMENTAL

Right: The cover for *Elemental* was the first full album in the 'solo' Tears For Fears period. (*Fontana/Mercury*)

Left: A still from the 'Goodnight Song' video. The single was given a limited release in the US and Canada. (*Fontana/ Mercury*)

TEARS FOR FEARS

+ RAOUL AND THE KINGS OF SPAIN +

Right: The album cover for *Raoul and the Kings of Spain.* The last 'solo' Tears For Fears album. (*Epic*)

Left: Roland singing 'Secrets' on Norwegian TV. It wasn't released as a single in the UK.

Right: The *Raoul and the Kings of Spain* era band playing 'Secrets' on Norwegian TV.

Left: Curt and Roland's reunion is marked by *Everybody Loves a Happy Ending.* There are similarities to *The Seeds of Love* cover. (*Gut/New Door*)

Right: The reunited duo performing 'Secret World' on the *Conan O'Brien Show.*

Below: A still of the pair taken from the *Secret World – Live in Paris* album and DVD. (*XIII Bis*)

Right: The band's distinctive sunflower imagery is front and centre on the first compilation album from 1992. (*Fontana/Mercury*)

Left: The band's only compilation of B-sides, extra tracks, and rarities. It also finds a home for their much-maligned single, 'The Way You Are'. (*Fontana/Mercury*)

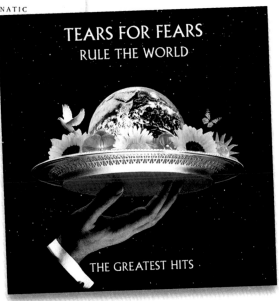

Right: The band's second official compilation album, it contained two bonus songs, the first new original material in 13 years. (*Virgin/EMI*)

Left: A limited-edition release and the band's contribution to Record Store Day 2014 was an EP of cover versions from contemporary artists. (*INgrooves*)

Left: The excellent Cinta Vidal cover artwork for 2022's universally praised *The Tipping Point*. (*Concord Records*)

Above: Curt and Roland performing on Radio 2's *Piano Room Sessions* in 2022. (*BBC*)

Below: Roland in the foreground and the band's keyboard player Doug Petty performing on Radio 2's *Piano Room Sessions* in 2022. (*BBC*)

Left: The first solo offering from Curt Smith. This has been forgotten by the artist but is liked in certain quarters by his fanbase. (*Phonogram*)

Right: The updated 2011 cover of the Curt Smith solo album Mayfield. (*Curt Smith Bandcamp*)

Left: In Canada *Aeroplane* was released as an album in 1999, in the US, it was released in 2000 as a six-track EP. (*Sour Music*)

Right: Curt Smith, the family man, is represented on the cover of the 2008 album, *Halfway, pleased.* (*Curt Smith Bandcamp*)

curt smith
halfway, pleased

Curt Smith | Deceptively Heavy

Left: The cover for the 2013 Curt Smith album, *Deceptively Heavy,* sees a mannequin clad in a Ben Sherman t-shirt, a brand much loved by the artist. (*Curt Smith Bandcamp*)

roland orzabal
tomcats screaming outside

Right: Roland Orzabal's only solo offering under his own name to date, sees him exploring the contemporary sounds of the day. (*Eagle*)

Above: Scenes from *The Tipping Point* tour. The intimate setting of the 02 Shepherds Bush Empire, July 2022. (*Paul Clark*)

Below: Curt from one of the last dates of the 2022 tour before it was cancelled due to a rib injury suffered by the singer. (*Paul Clark*)

Even though Orzabal had always been the principal songwriter in the band, the pressure increased for him to deliver now that he was the sole focus. There had been suggestions that Tears For Fears' name would be side-lined and for Orzabal to carry on under his name, but he joked that this was not an option because people could not pronounce it. The reality was all the more practical; the record label had invested a lot of time and money into the Tears For Fears brand and they still thought that this was a more viable option commercially. But even with the record company pressure, the use of the Tears For Fears name was not definite for this album. It was only when Orzabal got to the end of the recordings for *Elemental* and that he felt that it sounded like a Tears For Fears album that a final decision was made.

The split from Curt Smith saw Orzabal form another collaborative partnership that would prove fruitful through the next few albums. He wrote a great deal of the *Elemental* with Alan Griffiths, who had previously worked with the band, having been one of the guitarists on the *Songs from the Big Chair* tour. He had come to the attention of the band during his time with the band The Escape, who were label mates of TFF at Phonogram – they also had Nicky Holland as a touring keyboard player. Despite writing a lot of material during this period, he was never officially credited as a member of Tears For Fears, working on *Elemental* and *Raoul and the Kings of Spain*, as well as getting involved with the production of Orzabal's solo effort *Tomcats Screaming Outside* in 2001. Apart from Curt Smith, the partnership with Griffiths was one of the longest of Orzabal's career. Sadly, Alan passed away in 2017, at the age of 57. Talking about the process of writing collaboratively to *Songwriting Magazine* in 2022, Orzabal said:

When we started working together, I'd never really sat down with anyone in the studio with a blank slate. This was the beginning of the 90s and Al was coming in with his computer, we would sync up the computers and we'd just start jamming; improvising. And we got all of *Elemental* from that approach.

The first collaborations made it onto the B-sides and in the age of the CD single where more tracks were often needed than the old-fashioned 7-inch single and it was a chance to see how the band's sound had developed. A number of these tunes can be found on the *Saturnine Martial & Lunatic* album.

However, *Elemental* does feel more stripped back in terms of personnel. *The Seeds of Love* had a cast of thousands as the band employed the great and the good of the session world to record the album.

The themes of the new album covered the typical concerns of Orzabal that he had expressed on previous albums; the spiritual and the psychological. These themes could be channelled even more as he was now in charge of the band. Orzabal has been quoted by *Udiscovermusic.com* as saying that the album is about 'celebrating the fact that things do end. There's a cycle to life. Everything in the universe is recyclable – even you!'

The album feels like a crossroads and given the freedom Orzabal had of being in sole charge, there is no specific direction. The band embraced several styles again, as is the case with most Tears For Fears releases, moving further away from being the '80s band' that they are often misperceived as being. The album has hints of jazz, alongside the ever-luxuriously produced prog-pop that they had embraced on *The Seeds of Love*.

The cover is a photo of an Orzabal in a barren landscape; the colours are grey and frosty, while flames decorate the CD acknowledging Orzabal's star sign Leo, which has fire as its element.

Given the range of songs that appeared across the various formats available at the time of their release, there has yet to be a deluxe box set edition of the album. Extra songs may emerge down the line.

'Elemental' (Roland Orzabal, Alan Griffiths)

The first song on the album and in the post-Curt Smith period is an interesting marker as to how the sound of Tears For Fears would develop. The title is about getting back to basics and the opener does have a more simplistic feel to it. It is built around a rhythm track and guitar riff that builds throughout the song. It's constructed around a sample of a guitar using the wah-wah that is taken from one of the band's B-sides, 'Lord of Karma'. The song features an impassioned vocal from Orzabal, while the bassline and jangly guitars feel inspired by the Madchester sound that had been prevalent in the years before its release. The Stone Roses, The Charlatans, and The Happy Mondays were synonymous with this style of music – bands who mixed the jangly guitar sound of The Byrds with the emerging dance culture in the UK.

'Cold' (Roland Orzabal)

Highest chart places: UK: 72

The second single in the UK and the only song that was not a co-write. The song was inspired by an encounter with a German photographer on a previous tour. During a live performance, Orzabal was unwilling to be photographed, so he turned away from the camera. He received a note from her later on that read, 'how can someone who makes such warm music, be so cold?' Thematically, that was the starting point of the song, but the lyrics have multiple targets and it may also contain the first real dig at his erstwhile partner, via the bridge just before the first chorus, 'Time stood still with his fingers in his ears/Didn't want to hear it from another bunch of hollow men'. The second bridge also addresses the band's former manager Paul King, who had been jailed for stealing from the band. 'King got caught with his fingers in the till/Where's your calculator? Will you leave it in your will?' King would be convicted many years later for defrauding investors in a scam for a supposed cure for drunkenness which was made from volcanic rock. The lyrics of both bridges are not listed in the sleeve notes, but they can be heard quite clearly. He even references his old songwriting partner Nicky Holland, but this time more positively, 'Listened to my old Nockles/Hoped that it would warm the cockles'.

There are more astrological allusions with 'And Capricorn is rising, yes I'm cold'. In astrological terms, Capricorn is the start of the winter period – those born under that sign can be seen to be frosty, cold, and aloof.

Musically, it is a standard rock song, containing the customary combination of guitars, bass, and vocal and while other textures underpin the song the guitar dominates. The structure of the song again recalls the stylings of The Beatles, along with the backing harmonies that underpin the song, especially in the lead-up to the chorus.

When released as a single 'Cold', scraped into the charts at number 72 in the UK and dropped out the following week. Interestingly, the US record label did not release this as a single. Indeed, apart from 'Break it Down Again', the album did not contain many obvious singles, although 'Goodnight Song' was arguably a candidate and it was released in some territories, but not in the UK.

For the video, the setting is a bleak industrial building with the imposing presence of heavy machinery.

'Break It Down Again' (Roland Orzabal, Alan Griffiths)
Highest chart places: UK: 20, US: 25

This first single was an important signpost on the way forward for the band. No doubt there was a lot of pressure riding on it, but it delivered. Martial drumming opens up the song and returns towards the end to help to set this one up as a big number. There is a strong vocal from Orzabal, who is heartfelt in his belief about the new era, a new start. 'A lot of the songs were written while I was in a sense going through the 'divorce,' Orzabal told *The Washington Post* in 1993. 'Things like 'Break It Down Again' refer to that to some degree, and 'Fish Out of Water,' obviously. I did psychotherapy for about six years. I stopped regularly going when I'd finished *Elemental*, which I think probably says something. I think I'm moving on'. The cover of the single had a very metaphorical take on the band's state with Orzabal pictured in the desert holding a withered bunch of sunflowers. The Sunflower symbolism was something that was very much a part of the previous album's iconography – it was referred to on 'Sowing the Seeds of Love too. The cover alludes to that era being over. It has withered away, despite Orzabal's attempts to nurture it. It is interesting to note that the sunflower symbolism has been used again since Smith and Orzabal reformed, on tour t shirts and stage designs.

Although the overall subtext of the song is about the process of ageing, that might have a double meaning that leaves the song lyrically ambiguous: 'All the love in the world/won't stop the rain from falling' sets a pessimistic tone to the lyrics.

There is a widescreen video that accompanies the song that shows the video degrading. The image of the sleeve is replicated in the video, at desert El Mirage Lake, California, where the album covers were also taken.

It is a song that deserves to be judged as a Tears For Fears classic. It is a high watermark and has been ever-present on the setlists of the reunited Tears For Fears live gigs in recent years.

'Mr Pessimist' (Roland Orzabal, Alan Griffiths)

There is a sumptuous piano motif that runs throughout the song that recalls the work of Talk Talk. Very much in keeping with the style of Nicky Holland, there is a softly sung reflective vocal from Roland and a rumbling bassline, played by Guy Pratt, that runs throughout that recalls some of Pino Palladino's playing on *The Seeds of Love*.

Lyrically, it may well be another song that was aimed in the direction of Curt Smith. It could also be about Dr Arthur Janov, although they are probably about the passing of time and time running out. The 'Mr Pessimist' in question might also be Orzabal and the song could be reflective of his thoughts at the time of writing. It could well have started from the demo of 'My Life in the Suicide Ranks' a skeletal demo that first appeared as one of the extra tracks on the 'Women in Chains' single. The 'evangelistic brother should be banging a tambourine' line was first used in that song. 'Mr Pessimist' is quite an atmospheric, lengthy number. There is a sense of loss hanging over it, a feeling that is replicated across other parts of the album.

'Dog's a Best Friend's Dog' (Roland Orzabal, Alan Griffiths)

This is more of a guitar-led song. The big guitar figure at the start shows some of the sonic contrasts in the album. However, this falls into the rockier end of things, eschewing the typical Tears For Fears sound and is very much a rock song at a time when Grunge was breaking through. It's a reasonably interesting diversion, although lyrically it does not have an overall meaning, it does have several interesting lines, one including a reference to Samuel Beckett's play *Waiting for Godot* with the couplet 'Word, speech, blurred, bleached/ Tell Mr Godot I'm walking the dog, Walking the dog'. It's an interesting play on words.

'Fish Out of Water' (Roland Orzabal, Alan Griffiths)

Several songs on *Elemental* have subtle references to the break-up of the Smith/ Orzabal relationship, but 'Fish Out of Water' has no ambiguity about it. Line by line, it is an attack on Curt Smith. In the tradition of John Lennon firing lyrical barbs at his former partner Paul McCartney, this is Orzabal's, 'How Do You Sleep'.

It's not one of the better numbers on the album and it's fairly perfunctory musically. The song opens with a guitar, that fades into the background as the drum beat and piano motif carry on throughout the verses. The guitar comes and goes throughout the song before it returns at the end with a solo that leads the song to its fade.

Some fans would happily skip this track these days, especially now that the original partnership is back together. The feelings conveyed in this song are now water under the bridge, but it's quite a vitriolic attack on his former bandmate and it shows that a lot of ground had to be covered before they got back together eventually.

There are several astrological allusions in the lyrics. There are references to Smith's watery Cancerian nature. That may be one of the inspirations for the title as the first verse says, 'You always said you were the compassionate one'. Compassion is usually seen as a trait for Cancerians. They are also noted as being dreamers, referenced with 'you're dreaming your life away'.

The primal scream that they bonded over is referenced as a way of showing how both partners had moved away from their original ideals. Neptune's Kitchen is the home studio where Orzabal recorded much of this album. David Sinclair reviewing the song in *The Times* in 1993 described it as 'hilarious. He went to deride the couplet, suggesting how hard it is to take a man seriously when he sings: 'We used to sit and talk about primal scream/Now in Neptune's kitchen, you will be food for killer whales?'

Curt's response was equally cutting when he penned his song 'Sun King', which appears on the *Mayfield* album. In the song, Smith accused Orzabal of using astrology to justify his abusive behaviour. The title is a reference to Orzabal's star sign, Leo. 'Sun King' was a title used by Louis XIV. The French King was famous for being a tyrant. Smith painted Orzabal as a spiteful, narcissistic recluse, exhibiting signs of mental instability.

To be fair to Smith, there seem to be no hard feelings about the song, during a fan Q&A on Twitter a few years back, he was asked which Roland-era Tears For Fears song would he like to sing. No doubt, with his tongue placed firmly in his cheek when he composed his response, he suggested this one.

Smith talked about the song in a round of interviews promoting *The Tipping Point*:

It comes up in various conversations in a facetious way. Here's the joy of growing older: we know we've abused each other in worse ways than that in the past to each other's faces [laughs], so it doesn't matter in a song, other than a lot of people get to hear it!

Orzabal's reflected on the song in 2022 with a Q&A with NME. The song was was supposed tongue-in-cheek:

How can I abuse someone? 'Fish Out of Water' amused me at the time because I had left that behind and it didn't bother me that much. I was happy doing my own thing, so I found it amusing that a few years later, someone was still harking back to the anthem forgot about. It was it is an amusing back-and-forth that we now laugh about.

'Gas Giants' (Roland Orzabal, Alan Griffiths)
Tears For Fears have produced several atmospheric instrumentals down the years and this fits into that category. It feels like an interlude between one section of

the album and the next – a palate cleanser after the vitriol of the last song. It's akin to the more experimental numbers that have been released as B-sides down the years. The bassline and keyboard pattern run throughout the song and acts as the hook. Sonically, it may have been another song that takes its inspiration from Talk Talk. It recalls the slow-build atmospheric piano of 'April 5th'.

The title is the name of a giant planet composed mainly of hydrogen and helium. There is a short lyric towards the end which says 'Giants on Armistice Day/ Caught between the rock and the renegade'. It feels like a distant cousin of the instrumental track 'Listen' on *Songs from the Big Chair*, but without the epic quality of that track. Lyrically and musically, it feels quite amorphous.

'Power' (Roland Orzabal, Alan Griffiths)

This was one of the first things that Orzabal wrote in collaboration for the album. The song was written in response to the birth of his son. The lyrics in question relate to the birth and the power of the female. 'Power now is all the rage/ Sons and daughters of the gun/Hungry babies come of age'.

It's a song that has a slow build epic quality about it. There is a simplicity to the chorus, the refrain feels like it is a nod to the way that 'Shout' was constructed. The guitar solo is atmospheric and quite understated, but it is integral to the overall feeling of the song. The ending melds into the song that follows. This song in the middle of 'Gas Giants' and 'Brian Wilson Said' shows the power of sequencing a record. It feels like this suite of songs is delivering the listener to the payoff with the big, late-album number.

'Brian Wilson Said' (Roland Orzabal, Alan Griffiths)

Having captured The Beatles' sound so effectively on 'Sowing the Seeds of Love', 'Brian Wilson Said' does a good job of capturing the summery vibes of the Beach Boys. This perfectly observed imitation, blends into something akin to progressive jazz before coming back to the opening motif of the song to resolve the number. The verses that spell out the girl's names resonate with the Beach Boys' classic song 'California Girls', and in the way that the song shifts and shapes through the musical movements, there are hints of 'Good Vibrations'. There's a beautifully tender vocal from Orzabal that takes the song to the end. This is a gorgeous number and adds to the 60s influences that have been present on the Tears For Fears albums of later years. The title is a nod to the Van Morrison song 'Jackie Wilson Said', (later covered by Dexy's Midnight Runners, arguably the more famous of the versions), who wrote the song in tribute to one of his idols. Orzabal is paying tribute to one of his own with this track.

'Goodnight Song' (Roland Orzabal, Alan Griffiths)

Highest chart places: US: 125.
On 'Goodnight Song', Orzabal expresses abandonment and misunderstanding as he reflects on what has happened between him and Curt. The 'Goodnight Song' in question might be a reference to 'Everybody Wants to the Rule the

World'. This was a song that his former partner would have sung when the band played live. For all the emotions expressed in 'Fish Out of Water,' the song does reflect a sadness that things were no longer the same. Musically, there is a great guitar line that runs throughout the song, which creates a catchy hook.

It's a powerful song that would have made a great single if it had been given a proper release in the UK – a better choice than 'Cold', with the benefit of hindsight. Unreleased in the UK, it did chart in Canada and the US and there is a video on YouTube that shows the band in a live performance setting. The label had seemingly given up on their album at this point.

Stand Alone Singles, B-sides, EPs and Other Contemporary Tracks

Elemental has yet to be given the 'deluxe album' treatment as yet, but there are several B-sides and extra tracks from this period across the two singles. They can also be found on *Saturnine Martial & Lunatic* compilation.

'Elemental (Sons of August Mix)' (Roland Orzabal, Alan Griffiths)
The song was also released in France as a single in 1993
This remix of the opening track of the album, 'Elemental (Sons of August Mix)', is very rare indeed and can be found only on a French two-track CD single release. The remix accentuates the backbeat and the wah-wah guitar of the original song.

It might be hard to locate in physical form, but this mix can be heard on YouTube.

Raoul and the Kings of Spain

Personnel:
Roland Orzabal: Lead vocals, guitar, keyboards
Alan Griffiths: Guitar, keyboards
Jebin Bruni: Hammond organ
Gail Ann Dorsey: Bass guitar
Brian MacLeod: Drums, percussion
Jeffrey Trott: Guitar
Oleta Adams: Guest vocalist on 'Me and My Big Ideas'
Mark O'Donoughue: backing vocals
Record label: Sony/Epic Reissue: Cherry Red
Recorded: Tim Palmer, Roland Orzabal and Alan Griffiths
Release Date: 16th October 1995
Highest Chart Placings: UK: 41, US: 79
Run Time: 50:16

Raoul and the Kings of Spain is the final 'solo' Tears For Fears album and was released almost two years after *Elemental*, which is a quick turnaround when compared to the band's usual schedule. The album was very much a personal affair for the singer, with lyrical content that is as contemplative as you would expect for an Orzabal release. The introspection this time focuses on his family heritage with musical stylings reflective of his lineage. Orzabal has claimed that the album takes a back-to-basics approach, but it still has that lush production that has been a trademark of the band's previous output.

Commercially it was not the success that other Tears For Fears albums had been previously. The lack of sales may have been down to the more personal nature of the sound and the themes of the album, or it may have been the case that the music was out of step with the prevailing culture at the time. The album was released at the time of Britpop, just as Tears For Fears, ironically, had moved away from the 60s-infused pop of the previous albums to a more progressive sound. The direction of the music industry had moved towards a style that the band had moved away from. It was out of step with the times.

Critically it won favour in some places, but in others it was derided as being self-indulgent. *The Guardian's* Caroline Sullivan was one reviewer who wasn't a fan of the album:

> According to Roland Orzabal, who has run TFF since the departure of Curt Smith, this is a back-to-basics album. But his idea of 'basics' is any other outfit's idea of fantastic ornateness – *Raoul* ... is informed by washes of guitar, keyboard and Hammond organ, the whole thing as lush as a state-of-the-art studio could render it.

It was well-received amongst the band's fervent fanbase and it is still held in high regard today. The album might have made a more appropriate solo album under Roland Orzabal's name, given the style and the introspection present, but instead, it is was once again a Tears For Fears release. It's likely that this decision was out of his hands as he was in the process of swapping labels and Sony would no doubt have wanted the easier-to-market Tears For Fears brand.

Despite the issues with the label change, Orzabal found that there was a lot of ease in the creative process and talking to the *Tampa Bay Times* at the time of the album's release, he said:

> In the old days, I had to come up with a lot of things myself … kind of like the goose that laid the golden egg. It was a lot of pressure, and once you brought the songs in, a lot of arguing about how to do things in the studio. Now, working with (co-composer and co-producer) Alan Griffiths, there's no pressure.

The age-old issues with record labels came to the fore again. He was now signed to an American label and in their eyes, he was deemed to be an international artist and the label's enthusiasm was weakened as a result of that. So when the first single flopped, they abandoned the project in terms of promotion.

There had been plans for other songs to be released, but in the end, only the title track and 'Gods Mistake' was selected, resulting in diminishing returns in terms of sales and chart success

There are some quirks in the running order of earlier promotional releases of the album that collectors might be interested in as the band switched labels from Mercury / Polygram to Sony in 1995. Mercury had planned to release the album and had already issued advance promotional copies with a slightly different track listing. On the Mercury version, 'Queen of Compromise' is listed instead of 'Humdrum and Humble' and 'I Choose You.', which would appear on the eventual Sony release. According to Orzabal: 'I lived with the album for many months and although I have nothing against the track 'Queen of Compromise', I felt that the running order meant that the end wasn't as dynamic as the beginning. Inserting the two new tracks has made me extremely happy with the end product.' The song was issued as B-side and can now be found on the expanded version of the album.

There are three different versions of the record: the Sony 12-track original; a deluxe cigar box edition; and the 2009 Cherry Red edition. This latter version is the original release remastered, with five B-sides and acoustic versions of the tracks 'Raoul and the Kings of Spain' and 'Break it Down'. None of the B-sides/ extras was incorporated on the *Saturnine Martial & Lunatic* album as that collection was released by the band's previous label.

The cover image is from the famous Running the Bulls festival in Pamplona in Spain. Photographed by Jose Galle, it is titled 'Running Them in at Pamplona'.

'Raoul and the Kings of Spain' (Roland Orzabal, Alan Griffiths)
Highest chart places: UK: 31

References to Raoul and the Kings of Spain had cropped up several times throughout the career of Tears For Fears, and it was inevitable that the phrase would be incorporated into an actual album at some time, having been in the running for the title of the band's third album. There was a reference to the title when the band included it as a line in their cover of The Beatles 'All You Need is Love', which they played as a transition between 'The Seeds of Love' and 'Everybody Wants to Rule the World' on *The Seeds of Love* world tour. A version of that can be found on the band's 1990 DVD release, *Going to California*.

It's a track that had been around for a while, first appearing on the setlist on dates during the 1993 *Elemental world tour*. It's a guitar-driven number that is announced with a riff that features throughout the song. The bass and keyboards come in a few seconds later and emphasise the song's big arrangement.

The personal themes come to the fore and these are maintained across the rest of the album. Raoul was a name that Orzabal assigned at birth until his mother decided on the more Anglicised Roland two weeks later. But it's a name that has been in the family for many generations, he retained it as a nickname and gave it to his first son.

The Kings of Spain is a reference to his family lineage on his father's side. His father was of Spanish-Basque descent, and his grandfather was Argentinian. His father had told him that his great-great-grandmother was the cousin of the president of Argentina., implying, of course, that the song and album should have been called Raoul and the Presidents of Argentina'. But as Orzabal observed at the time, 'not a lot of things rhyme with Argentina'.

The video for the song was filmed at The Mission Inn Hotel & Spa in Riverside, California and features the touring band, including Orzabal, Alan Griffiths and bassist Gail Ann Dorsey.

'Falling Down' (Roland Orzabal)
This is a catchy number with an affecting riff that chimes away throughout the intro and the verses. The chorus gives way to something powerful and rockier. Two songs in and the album is shaping up to be dominated by guitars with this track sounding like another that comes from a live setting rather than being conceived in the studio as their previous releases had been. It's a song that has been performed occasionally by the band in its current, third incarnation.

The lyrics may be reflective of Orzabal's attitude towards himself at the time, questioning his lot: 'Some of us are saints/Some are clowns/Just like me, they're falling down'. In a radio interview in 1995, Orzabal did use the analogy of President Nixon, who had spent his life striving for something and when he achieved it, he found that t wasn't all that he wanted it to be, paralleling the singer and his position in the music business at the time. Indeed, in terms of chart success and sales, Orzabal was a long way from where he was in the mid-80s. He may have been content creatively, but his label will also have had issues with the numbers that the releases were achieving.

The song was issed as a limited promotional radio-only single in the US, Brazil, Mexico, and some European countries, but not in the UK., as an alternative to 'Secrets', which had only been released in some territories.

'Secrets' (Roland Orzabal, Alan Griffiths)

Highest chart places. USA: DNC

This is a beautifully haunting piano-led song that shows the variation across the album. It is a nice contrast from the two rockier opening tracks, having a great riff that acts as the hook in the chorus. The vocals are impeccable as ever and the downward chord pattern of the verse has a Lennonesque quality. The emotive vocal in the middle eight is set against a big, radio-friendly guitar solo.

The song was also planned to be released in the UK as a two-part single, but was withdrawn, only released in the US and throughout parts of Europe with little commercial success. There are also two videos for the single; the first one was shot in late 1995, but Orzabal was not happy with how it turned out. The second version is made up of a collage of people's faces interspersed with shots of Orzabal and his family, including his first wife, Caroline, who appears painting on a canvas. She had previously appeared in the *Sowing the Seeds of Love* video.

'God's Mistake' (Roland Orzabal, Alan Griffiths)

Highest chart places: UK:61, US:102.

Another song that mines another of Orzabal's interests and turns it into an archetypical pop song. It was the second single to be taken from the album in the UK, faring modestly. In an age of Oasis, it's unlikely that the wider populace was not looking for a song about quantum mechanics. It was the first single taken from the album in the United States and also in Canada, where it was a minor hit.

It's a good song in the context of the whole of the album, but, understandably, it was perceived to have some commercial potential. Again, it has a more organic, live band feel to it and the song is less ornate than previous singles, with the guitars to the fore, but in perhaps a more restrained way than the rest of the album.

Lyrically the song comes from a period in Orzabal's life when he was reading a great deal on new physics and parapsychology. One of the ideas that he latched on to was the quote from Albert Einstein from The Born-Einstein Letters, published in 1971, 'I, at any rate, am convinced that [God] does not throw dice'.

In an interview at the time, Orzabal told science writer Paul Halpern:

I took this idea of God sitting there and designing the universe in a very mechanical way, such that if you knew the starting point of every particle, you knew the result, the outcome. So, therefore, 90% of human subjective experience — with love being a very important one, love which defies gravity, and breaks Einsteinian speed limits — must be a mistake. Because it doesn't fit in with the divine plan; it's illogical.

Orzabal would again reference God playing dice on the song 'Hey Andy' from his solo album *Tomcats Screaming Outside*.

The video has that sheen to it that suggests it was produced ostensibly for the US market. The live band play in the desert, while other clips are interspersed into the footage of a Vegas-style casino.

'Sketches of Pain' (Roland Orzabal)

This is a beautifully ornate song, highlighting the different textures across the album. The song opens with an acoustic finger-picked pattern that continues throughout the verse. Then other flourishes are introduced to build what is quite an intricate song. It is certainly in keeping with the tone of the album, but it is a style that has not been associated with Tears For Fears before. The flamenco part towards the end gives the song a lift before a return to the main melody. The title is a play on the title of the Miles Davis album *Sketches of Spain* and given the Spanish theme of the album and the notable flamenco stylings, the reference is quite apt. The song is supposedly about Vincent Van Gogh – an attempt to evoke the atmosphere of his paintings through music.

'Los Reyes Católicos' (Roland Orzabal, Alan Griffiths)

The phrase Los Reyes Católicos translates as 'the Catholic Kings' in Spanish, and it's the title of the song that acts as a bridge between more substantial tracks while continuing the theme of the album. The first part of the song (the bulk of it is reprised at the end of the album) is a sparsely arranged number. The instrumentation is mainly a lightly strummed guitar, with a slow building atmospheric bed of keyboards in the background. The vocals are treated and have an eerie, haunting quality to them.

'Sorry' (Roland Orzabal, Alan Griffiths)

Following on from the calm and reflective previous track, this is quite a guitar-heavy number, with a more subtle shift in the chorus to something more contemplative. The piano motif is a nice counterpoint to the full-on, rockier guitar lines. But it all feels a little routine and is not one of the memorable tracks on the album. The song asks, 'Do you love or do you hate? Why do you hesitate?' – another song that may be reflective of the state of Orzabal's life and relationships at the time.

'Humdrum and Humble' (Roland Orzabal, Alan Griffiths)

This mid-tempo rocker had the potential to be another good single for the band. 'Sorry' almost segues into the song as Orzabal sings, 'Cut, spite, face', then finally just 'Cut', before offering a seamless transition to this track. The intro has the guitar panning across both channels – clearer if you listen to the song on headphones.

This song was one of the additions to the Sony release and the album is all the better for its inclusion as it's a brisk number with a decent pop hook, if lyrically, it's hard to pin down.

'I Choose You' (Roland Orzabal)
Tears For Fears albums always have elements of introspection and this is one of the tenderest moments on the album. There is a beautiful Orzabal vocal that is accompanied by piano. At the time, it was felt like this might have been one of the last songs to be recorded under the Tears For Fears name, and it certainly marks the end of the Roland Orzabal-helmed version of the band. Overall, this is another fine song that fits in with this album. There is a reference to 'the kitchen', which could be Neptune's Kitchen, Roland's home studio, which was previously referenced on 'Fish Out of Water'. It's another bridge between the heavier songs on the album.

'Don't Drink the Water' (Roland Orzabal, Alan Griffiths)
Amongst the introspection and the subtle moments, 'Don't Drink the Water' is an out-and-out foot on the monitor rocker. It opens with a piano riff, crashing car samples and colliding guitars. Roland's vocals throughout the verse are almost spoken, as he acts as the narrator of this tale. The 'don't drink the water' refrain feels more like a middle eight than a chorus, as it gets repeated throughout the song and there is a great riff running through the song that breaks down at the end with a big solo. A great live track, potentially, but it was only played during the tours following the release of the album. The lyrics reference the Mexican painter Frida Kahlo, famous for her self-portraits. While this is not about her specifically, it's one of several songs on the album that references artworks or artists.

'Me and My Big Ideas' (Roland Orzabal, Alan Griffiths)
The song reunites Orzabal with Oleta Adams for the first time since *The Seeds of Love*. It's a big production; a call and response number. The production is as multifaceted as you would expect for a Tears For Fears release. Oleta Adams comes in on the third verse. The song feels like a call back to 'Head Over Heels' from *Songs from the Big Chair* by mentioning a 'four-leaf clover'. Arguably the band's first out-and-out 'love song', the accompanying video showed the start of a relationship and flashforward to a time when the writer would be older and settled. The four-leaf clover in 'Me and My Big Ideas' is being blown away and it is symbolic of the end of a relationship or one that is struggling. The 'So many strings to your bow, why not let one go' may be addressing his wife. It's raw and emotional and feels like an album closer, given its intensity.

'Los Reyes Católicos' (Reprise) (Roland Orzabal, Alan Griffiths)

The last track on the album is a reprise of track number six. It follows the same template, but it is substantially longer. The outro is a repeat of the 'the ghosts are gone' lyric with an atmospheric, percussion-heavy sound. It's all more textured than the first inclusion of the song and acts as a gentle exit from the album.

Stand Alone Singles, B-sides, EPs and Other Contemporary Tracks

Although these tracks were released before *Saturnine Martial & Lunatic*, the following songs never made it to that collection of B-sides and rarities as that collection bundled up the songs from the Mercury/Phonogram years. These *Raoul*-era songs could be found in the singles at the time, which was the era of multiple formats and two different CD versions of the same track – the short-lived CD single double set, which led to bands at the time writing and releasing a greater number of tracks. It was good for the fans, but not great for those songwriters who were put under more pressure to come up with material.

'Creep' (Live) (Thom Yorke, Colin Greenwood, Philip Selway, Jonny Greenwood, Ed O'Brien)

One of the more interesting songs that come from this period is the release of the live version of Radiohead's 'Creep'. Tears For Fears have played cover versions live down the years, but this song had been an integral part of their set for some time, both before and after Curt Smith returned to the band. So often had they played it, that it felt like they were claiming it as their own. Radiohead released it in 1992 and that band stopped playing it, although it has crept back into their set on recent tours.

The Tears For Fears cover appeared as an extra track in 1995 as a B-side of 'Raoul and the Kings of Spain'. This live version is a fairly faithful take on the original, the only lyrical embellishment being the inclusion of the place where the gig was taking place that night, which sounds like NEC, Birmingham. It was recorded on a date on *The Raoul and the Kings of Spain* tour. The song didn't make the setlist for the early dates on *The Tipping Point* world tour.

'Queen of Compromise' (Roland Orzabal, Alan Griffiths, Brian Macleod, Jebin Bruni, Gail Anne Dorsey, Jeffrey Trott)

The alternate track listing of the Mercury release had this as part of the album. After a few changes to the running order and the move to the new label it was relegated to the B-side of 'Raoul and the Kings of Spain' single. It's a decent mid-tempo of song, so is unlucky to have not made the final album. Again, guitars are to the fore. There does not seem to be an overall message in the song, but there are some arresting couplets. 'It happens all the time/I read your mind/Where dreams take second place/I'll invade your space/Your secrets will be mine'.

'What's your sign?' This is another reference to Orzabal's astrological interests. It's also the part of the song where Orzabal has a go at aping the vocal stylings of Gary Numan at 2:25 minutes into the song. Given the weightier themes of the album, perhaps it was left off due to its lightweight lyrical themes. The multiple co-writers with the touring band and the live-sounding nature of the song suggest that this was worked up by the live band.

'All the Angels' (Roland Orzabal, Alan Griffiths)
This is a bright number driven by a strummed guitar and it's another B-side from the 'Raoul and the Kings of Spain' single. It's another song concerning death; all of the angels are calling us home. That was something that was in Orzabal's thoughts at the time as a number of his extended family had had health issues, though sonically it sounds like Orzabal had been listening to a lot of Britpop bands. This is contrasted with a few Americanisms in the lyrics, especially the way he pronounces some of the words, 'leisure' for instance. It's another good vocal performance from Orzabal, although it does feel like he is buried in the mix a little

'The Madness of Roland' (Roland Orzabal, Alan Griffiths)
Another B-side from the 'Raoul and the Kings of Spain' single. The opening drums sound like the 'My Life in the Suicide Ranks' demo, but the atmospheric backing is in parts like 'Listen'. It's very much like Pink Floyd – big on ambience. This comes from the tradition of interesting Tears For Fears B-sides, where they take a much more experimental approach. The title may have been inspired by Greg Roach's multimedia book *The Madness of Roland*, presented as a CD Rom and not in the traditional printed form. It had elements of game-like interactivity that drive the narrative.

'Until I Drown' (Roland Orzabal, Alan Griffiths)
Opening up with a delicately finger-picked acoustic guitar, the lyrics seem to have Orzabal contemplating his lot again, 'Days are all the same/They wax and wane/I will be here until I drown'. This builds to a bigger arrangement that covers the same lyrical ground and builds to a nice fade. It's another B-side from the 'Gods Mistake' single and could easily have been on the album itself, although it may have missed out as it was too close in tone to 'I Choose You', but it's great all the same.

'War of Attrition' (Roland Orzabal, Alan Griffiths)
One of the other extras from the 'Gods Mistake' single. This opens with a metronomic beat and a piano before the rest of the band kicks in. It's a song that doesn't have any grand narrative, so it may have been inspired by the interesting title alone. It has some diverting sonic elements, with treated vocals over the middle eight and a piano motif running throughout.

'Raoul and the Kings of Spain' (Acoustic Version) (Roland Orzabal, Alan Griffiths)

This is an excellent live acoustic version of the title track song taken from BBC Radio 2's *Johnnie Walker Show*, from September 1995 and this is another B-side from the 'Gods Mistake' single. It's a fairly faithful version, with Orzabal backed by another guitarist with a light percussive element, showing off Orzabal's vocals quite well.

'Break it Down Again' (Acoustic Version) (Roland Orzabal, Alan Griffiths)

This is a live acoustic version of the *Elemental* song taken from the same radio session in September 1995. This is another B-side from the 'Gods Mistake' single. It seems a more laid-back version of the 1993 hit single, and breaking down the song to its purest essence offers up a great version of the song. It's an insight into the development of such a song. Even though Orzabal has been known to use the studio and technology to write songs, he has also used the traditional methods of just a guitar, going back even back to the days of *The Hurting*. The acoustic version is fairly faithful to the original, apart from the inclusion of the 'no more walls of Berlin' line.

Everybody Loves a Happy Ending

Personnel:
Roland Orzabal: Guitars, keyboards, lead vocals
Curt Smith: bass, keyboards, backing vocals, lead vocals
Charlton Pettus: Guitars, keyboards
Fred Eltringham: Drums
Brian Geltner: Drums
Rick Baptist: Trumpet
Kenny Siegal: Guitar, backing vocals
Gwen Snyder: Backing vocals
Alexander Giglio: Backing vocals
Julian Orzabal: Crowd vocals
Laura Gray: Crowd vocals
Paul Buckmaster: Orchestra arrangement and conducting
Bob Becker: Viola, Charlie Bisharat: Violin, Denyse Buffman: Viola, Eve Butler:
Violin, Mario de Leon: Violin, Joel Derouin: Violin, Stefanie Fife: Cello, Armen
Garabedian: Violin, Berj Garabedian: Violin, Barry Gold: Cello, Gary Grant:
Trumpet, flugelhorn, Maurice Grants: Cello, Julian Hallmark: Violin, Vahe
Hayrikyan: Cello, Norm Hughes: Violin, Suzie Katayama: Cello, contracting,
Roland Kato: Viola, Peter Kent: Violin, Steve Kujala: Flute, Gayle Levant: Harp,
Michael Markman: Violin, Miguel Martinez: Cello, Robert Matsuda: Violin, Carole
Mukogawa: Viola, Sid Page: Violin, Sandra Park: Violin, bSara Parkins: Violin,
Joel Peskin: Baritone saxophone, tenor saxophone, Bob Peterson: Violin, Karie
Prescott: Viola, Dan Smith: Cello, Rudy Stein: Cello, Lesa Terry: Violin, Josefina
Veraga: Violin, David Washburn: Trumpet, flugelhorn, Evan Wilson: Viola
John Wittenberg: violin ('Secret World')
Record label(s): New Door (US) Gut Records (UK)
Recorded: Tears For Fears, Charlton Pettus
UK Release Date: 7 March 2005
US Release Date 14 September 2004
Highest Chart Placings: UK: 45, US: 46
Run Time: 54:35

Nine years since the last Tears For Fears record and 15 since the last one to
feature Curt and Roland together, the band, (and their legions of fans) got their
Hollywood Ending in the form of the album *Everybody Loves a Happy Ending*.
The title started as something of a joke, but soon stuck. It says, 'hello we're
back. Have you missed us?'

After a period of little contact between the pair, apart from the occasional
business-related discussion, they reconvened in 2000 to rekindle the
partnership. They had always had mutual interests from the early days, but it
did not seem likely that a musical reconciliation would ever happen. That was
until a fax message appeared on Orzabal's printer with a telephone number
asking for him to get in touch with his former partner. Friends had been trying

to get the pair back together again, but this was the spark for the reunion. After making they made contact, Curt visited the UK and the pair decided to sit down to talk about music.

Curt brought along Charlton Pettus, who had been instrumental in helping Smith rekindle his love of music and who worked on Curt's solo albums. Pettus is still a member of the band today, contributing to songwriting and production.

There was a more organic approach to songwriting than had gone before. Curt and Roland sat down to write with acoustic guitars with Pettus at the upright piano waiting around for inspiration to strike. The band were undecided about which direction to go in; whether it was to follow a more contemporary rhythm-based approach favoured by Orzabal or to write something classic and melodic, as was Curt's desire – something that was in keeping with what the band had produced previously. Indeed, Orzabal's last release was the solo *Tomcats Screaming Outside* album, which was big on rhythm and influenced by contemporary artists such as Massive Attack and Portishead. But it was Curt's approach that won out.

It is clear from listening to the album that it was a happy period for the band. Orzabal told *HMV* when they released *The Tipping Point*: 'Pretty much the entire narrative of that album was just about us getting back together hence the gag: everybody loves a happy ending'.

It took a while for the album to come together, in that which time Orzabal moved his family over to the USA from England while the album was being written and produced. Orzabal reflected on the experience when he spoke to *HMV.com* in 2022.

That album was a journey, it was exciting. I took my family across to L.A., relocated them, and bought a house. It was a total change of lifestyle, which was needed, and my kids were still young enough that we could take them out of school and put them in L.A. It was doing the school run under blue skies, then straight onto the tennis court and into the recording studio. It was divine. But that album kind of reflects how easy it was because it's generally a pretty happy album, I would say.

There is a mix of sounds, all inspired by UK bands. There's a bit of Blur, The Jam, XTC, Madness and the ever-present influence of The Beatles. The sophisticated levels of production on the album bring to mind Jeff Lynne's ELO too. As ever, with a Tears For Fears release, the production is layered and lush.

The band acknowledge that is the album that might have followed *The Seeds of Love* if the pair had remained together. Having suppressed The Beatles influence for the Orzabal TFF albums, that style is to the fore here. In terms of the production and songwriting, this has Paul McCartney as a strong influence.

The artwork is a nod toward *The Seeds of Love*. The ornate, slightly psychedelic cover resonates with the style and sound of the band here. The Beatles influence can be seen here too.

Before the album came out, the band had to contend with record label issues. This seems often to be the case with the release of Tears For Fears albums in the latter part of their career. The album was due to appear on the Arista label in 2003, but a number of the label's management team left before any of the songs could see that light of day. Arista did release red vinyl promo copies and these are extremely rare, occasionally available on resale sites Discogs and eBay.

Critically the album received some good review reviews, the UK monthly publication *Uncut* described the album as being 'a guilty, gleeful indulgence'. It is an album that is appreciated by die-hard fans, even if It did not bring in a legion of new followers, with the band at the time feeling that they were not given the level of respect they deserved.

The band acknowledge that the record did not set the world alight when it was released and at the time, it was felt that the album may be the last collection of new songs from the band. They would just continue to tour. Smith reflected on the album in 2022 with *HMV*, just before the release of *The Tipping Point*:

We thought it was a good way to end, I think. It was more a celebration than anything, I mean there are some songs with depth on the album, but it's certainly not as deep as this one [*The Tipping Point*].

Roland Orzabal's summation of the album when talking to Paul Sinclair in 2022 was that:

… it was a beautiful, Beatle-y pop record, but [it was] lacking a little bit… Lacking the blood and guts. Lacking any sense of catharsis.

The album may have a new lease of life in the coming years, especially given the interest in *The Tipping Point* and the fact that the album was only introduced to streaming platforms in 2020. Meanwhile, a vinyl version of the album is much requested amongst the band's fanbase. It may get the super deluxe reissue treatment in the fullness of time, which might see it re-evaluated.

'Everybody Loves a Happy Ending' (Roland Orzabal, Curt Smith, Charlton Pettus)
Highest chart places: UK: 102
The 60s references are writ large throughout this number. The song exists as if the 1990s never happened. The opener and other parts of the album ignore the two Roland Orzabal era albums and act as a continuum of the sound of *The Seeds of Love* album.

As a pop song with movements, it's very progressive, as you might expect from the band, taking you in one direction, and then in another. There is a minute of intro - omitted from the edits of the single – that gives way to the piano-led chorus. There is a marked difference between the version that appears on the album and the one that was released as a double a-side (with 'Call Me Mellow') – the Steve Fitzmaurice mix is two minutes shorter and starts with the alarm clock and piano break – quite a brutal edit of the single given the form that the album version takes, even though the original 4:21 – is shorter than a number of the band's previous singles.

There's a Beatlesque, mellower acoustic interlude in the middle before the song returns to the 'wake up' element. It ramps up again to the big chorus and the hook to the end. As ever, an excellent bassline from Curt Smith that underpins the song and several 'woo-hoo' elements add to the number of the Paul McCartneyisms throughout the album. The song acts as a full-on Beatles tribute, in a similar vein 'Sowing the Seeds of Love', It crams a lot into its running time. Indeed, it feels longer, not because of its lack of quality, but because of the musical twists and turns, it takes. It was the second song from the album to be released as a single, but it failed to make an impact on the UK charts, where it landed no higher than 102.

'Closest Thing to Heaven' (Roland Orzabal, Curt Smith, Charlton Pettus)

Highest chart places: UK:40.

This was one of the first things that the trio wrote for the album and showed the potential of the songwriting team of Orzabal, Smith, & Pettus. The strident piano is the key element of the song, providing a theme that runs throughout the song and acts as its hook. It's another intricate progressive pop song that has all the elements that an expansive Tears For Fears single should have.

Curt's vocals stay in the background throughout the verses, but he contributes yet another understated bassline and he does get to sing the chorus, not unlike in his contributions to 'Sowing the Seeds of Love'.

Having done McCartney on the first song, the drumming throughout is very reminiscent of Ringo Starr. There's a bit of a reversed drum pattern just before the middle eight to complete the Ringoisms, while there are good harmonies between Orzabal and Smith throughout, which reminds the listener of what was lacking on the two previous Curt-free Tears For Fears albums. There seems to be some alchemy when the pair come together and this song reinforces that belief.

The video has yet more allusions to Orzabal's interest in all things astrological. Fire meets water with the Leo (Orzabal), reconciling with the Cancerian (Smith). The day and night, sun and moon, recall some of the themes that appeared throughout *The Seeds of Love* album. The late Brittany Murphy appears in this fantastical video directed by Michael Palmieri.

The lead single from the album, there is a 'Radio Mix' of the song that has brightened the tone even more. The single version is edited down to the barest detail and kicks off with the piano, omitting the ambient noise that the album version opens with. There are also several 'dance' remixes that are instantly forgettable. Sadly, the days of extra tracks and B-sides to keep the fans happy were seemingly no more, but it's another strong song that sits well on the *Rule the World* compilation album.

'Call Me Mellow' (Roland Orzabal, Curt Smith, Charlton Pettus)
Highest chart places: UK: 102.
While the melody has some similarities with 'There She Goes' by The La's. You could also throw in a bit of ELO, XTC's Dukes of the Stratosphere project, (and XTC themselves) and Jellyfish into the mix; it's another psychedelic pop song.

The album is full of sunny vibes and this is maybe reflective of the positivity that stems from the reformation and the fact that the album was recorded in LA. The intro has Curt Smith calling out to 'fill the sky with love', while the song has a simple arrangement with a jangly guitar building to a very catchy chorus. The vocal harmonies are as exemplary as ever.

The song was released as a double a-side, with 'Everybody Loves a Happy Ending'. This version has no edits, although there is an extra 'Tin Tin Out Vocal Mix' of the song, which is an interesting diversion from the original.

'Size of Sorrow' (Roland Orzabal)
This is probably the oldest song on the album. It has a solo Orzabal writing credit, mainly because it's something that predates their reformation. It had previously been performed live on the *Elemental* tour with the then vocalist/ bassist Gail Ann Dorsey singing the lead, although the lyrics have been altered for the version that appears on this album. Even though it's an Orzabal-penned song it sounds like it could be from one of Smith's solo later period releases, having a trademark tender Smith vocal, much missed during his absence from the band.

It starts with some electronic percussion that runs throughout the song that recalls *The Hurting* era, it also has echoes of Orzabal's work on his solo album, but the song then morphs into something typical of latter-day Tears For Fears. The backing is quite mellow. As a song, it doesn't stand out from the pack, but as part of the body of work, it's worthy of its place.

'Who Killed Tangerine?' (Roland Orzabal, Curt Smith, Charlton Pettus)
The drum pattern at the start and throughout the verse is, again, reminiscent of Ringo Starr, in particular, his work on 'Come Together' and the song has a descending chord pattern that has a noticeably 60s feel to it, with Curt Smith doing a mean Paul McCartney impression with his bassline. It is probably the song on the album that's most influenced by the Beatles. There is even a 'Hey Jude' style chorus that builds towards the end with the 'when you think it's all-over/it's not over' refrain. It has an orchestral element to reinforce the ambitious nature of the arrangement and further nods to its influences.

It's a song that was designed to be played live and to get the crowd singing along, although as they have a few of those in their back catalogue, it would probably explain why this song does not get rolled out more often than it does in a live setting.

The lyrics are ambiguous and we don't get to find out who actually killed Tangerine.

'Quiet Ones' (Roland Orzabal)

It's one of the few guitar-driven tracks on the album. It's quite straightforward, but it does have a subtle shift in gear for the bridge and chorus. The verses have a distorted vocal, but for the bridge and chorus, the vocals are more natural. The vocals are a masterclass in Orzabal's range and control, as he shifts from the more powerful delivery in the verses and bridge, which then gives way to the softer, almost feminine tones of the bright chorus. The harmonies tumble out and there are some effective guitar lines throughout this mid-tempo, rockier number.

There is a reference to 'another dead beetle' or is it Beatle? The quiet one was George Harrison's nickname, but there is nothing in the lyrics that suggests that this is a tribute to him specifically.

'Who You Are' (Curt Smith, Charlton Pettus)

This was something that also appears on the Curt Smith solo album *Halfway, Pleased*. It was the first original song that the band had released that did not have an Orzabal songwriting credit.

Curt sings this one with its delicate arrangement. This being a Tears For Fears song, it does not follow in the obvious direction that its mellower arrangement would suggest and there are a few diversions to keep the listener interested. There's a bit of Beatle-esque backward guitar in the interlude. The refrain/playout has a flashback and partial reprise of the 'wake up' element from 'Everybody Loves a Happy Ending'. This song marks the start of a more serene section of tracks on the album.

'The Devil' (Roland Orzabal)

This is a piano-led song that has minimal backing in its opening stages. Orzabal sings enthusiastically as he contemplates his fate and he faces up to his demons. The slow build is reminiscent of Lennon's 'I Want You/She's So Heavy' on Abbey Road in the way the dynamics as the song builds to its climax. Throw in some backward psychedelic guitar, and some fairground-style keyboards (buried in the mix) and you have a very evocative number. The song unspools and fades away at the end.

'Secret World' (Roland Orzabal)

This is the highlight of the album. This piano-led number comes replete with a big orchestrated score and guitar solos. When Tears For Fears want to throw the kitchen sink at a song they certainly do not hold back. In the past, they would have run this through a Fairlight, but the sleeve notes point to a cast of hundreds employed on a song that sounds all the more organic for this approach and the result justifies the time and expense taken.

While there are some good songs spread across the album, the reformation is certainly worth it for this track alone. A trickle-down piano at the start has echoes of the opening to 'Head Over Heels'. And there is a great vocal from Orzabal throughout that showcases his range.

Again, the Beatlesisms are to the fore with the arrangement that remains a mainstay of the band's set today. Live, the elongated instrumental section is given over to incorporating Paul McCartney's song, 'Let Me In'. There are many songs from their back catalogue that could be described as being 'accomplished', but this could be the most accomplished song of their career.

Lyrically, the song may be a call back to 'Advice for the Young at Heart', with 'too many people living in a secret world'. The thematic links to that song include growing up and getting lost in a secret world without paying attention to the process of ageing.

At the end of the song, you can hear Smith (or someone else) talking to the orchestra and thanking them. They deserve that acknowledgement. The band do too. This is a great track.

'Killing with Kindness' (Roland Orzabal, Curt Smith, Charlton Pettus)

After the epic nature of the previous track, the next one is a chance for the listener to catch their breath. It has a lullaby quality to it, with a mellow verse, which follows the descending chord pattern until the bridge, which then shifts up a gear. The chorus is as big and bold as you would expect from the band. But it's an understated song that has seemingly improved with age – the ultimate slow burner. If you have not heard the album in a while, it's worth paying attention to specifically. There's a lengthy outro that feels like the song is waving the listener off before the chorus comes back in, but It's such a good chorus that it's worth repeating.

'Ladybird' (Roland Orzabal, Curt Smith, Charlton Pettus)

This was one of the first songs that came together for the album. Curt and Charlton had the basis of the chorus written and when Orzabal heard that he added the melody and the lyrics. It opens with an Orzabal vocal and lightly strummed guitar, with background effects that slowly emerge as the song plays out. There's a nice outro that, again, like the previous song, feels like it's coming to its end but there is another twist. It is a deceptively simplistic track, although the time signatures do shift in the chorus to belie that simplicity. The chorus has two bars of 5/8, one bar of 9/8, two bars of 5/8, and ten bars of 6/8, while the main part of the song is in standard 6/8.

Lyrically the song is inspired by the old English language nursery rhyme, 'Ladybird, Ladybird'.

'Last Days on Earth' (Roland Orzabal, Curt Smith, Charlton Pettus)

This is a nice mellow closer to the album. Having asked us to pay attention to the cradle or the grave in 'Secret World', this song now seems to ponder the endpoint of life. It's a nice conceptual call back to 'Famous Last Words' on 'The Seeds of Love'. There's an almost childlike piano riff that opens the song and plays throughout, while the lyrics suggest a love song, but there are darker overtones at its heart. There is a big middle eight plus another great vocal from Orzabal that recalls David Bowie at his finest. It's a great way to end a great album.

Stand Alone Singles, B-sides, EPs and Other Contemporary Tracks

Given the problems with the release and the subsequent versions of the album, most of the extras are remixes of the singles. But the album did initially come with editions that had bonus tracks on the UK, Italian and French releases. These editions and songs are difficult to find in standard form, although they can be found on YouTube. Following the release of *The Tipping Point,* there is talk of a vinyl release and a possible deluxe edition of *Everybody Loves a Happy Ending*, but these have yet to see the light of day at the time of writing.

'Pullin' a Cloud' (Roland Orzabal, Gail Anne Dorsey, Brian MacLeod)

The co-writes on this one suggest that the song predates Smith re-joining as it was written by members of the previous touring band. It's different in tone from the rest of the album, so it is understandable that it's been consigned to the bonus tracks. It's predominately a finger-picked acoustic number and it's a gentle countrified number, it feels like something that could have found a home on the *Raoul on the Kings of Spain* album. There is minimal percussion and bassline in the middle eight before it returns to the main melody and the song has a tender and vulnerable vocal from Orzabal. It might not have fit the overall narrative of the album, but it deserved to be released as it's a bit of a lost gem.

'Out of Control' (Roland Orzabal, Curt Smith, Charlton Pettus, Alan Griffiths)

This was another of the bonus tracks available on the UK release of *Everybody Loves a Happy Ending*. As it doesn't feel that it has been fully realised, so it could be a demo recording. It's a tender number that, while it goes in a conventional direction, seems to throw in several quirky musical flourishes. It's deceptively hooky as it builds to an interesting finish. It's another song that references Frida Kahlo.

Ready Boy & Girls? EP

Personnel:
Roland Orzabal: producer, vocals, instruments
Curt Smith: vocals, instruments
Record label: INgrooves
Recorded: Tears For Fears and Charlton Pettus
Release Date: 19th April 2014
Highest Chart Placings: US DNC
Run Time: 12.02

It was hearing New Zealander Lordes' (of the 'Royale') version of 'Everybody Wants to Rule the World' recorded for the soundtrack of *The Hunger Games: Catching Fire* that encouraged Curt and Roland back to the studio in 2013. The idea was that the band would work on some cover versions to try and kick-start their writing.

Originally the songs were made available in 2013 on Soundcloud as a prelude for the release of new material, where they were well received by the band's fanbase eager for new songs. They were released in 2014 as a Record Store Day exclusive 10' vinyl EP called *Ready Boy and Girls?*, which was only released in the US, much to the frustration of UK fans and other international supporters.

Curt Smith told *Stereogum* in 2022 of the inspiration behind the selections:

We had no new material of our own at that point of time. So, you could do cover versions, but picking cover versions of our era was dull. As we've discussed, there were a lot of younger musicians who were sampling us or covering us, so we basically just thought we'd return the favour. That was the simple idea behind it. We went surfing around to find songs that spoke to us, and those were the ones that spoke to us.

Curt and Roland had previously released cover versions of Robert Wyatt's 'Sea Song', Radiohead's 'Creep', and David Bowie's 'Ashes to Ashes'. These are referenced elsewhere in the book, but these newer covers try to do something different from the originals, and no doubt fans looked to these tracks as a clue as to the direction that the band would take with their new album.

'My Girls' (Brian Weitz, David Portner, Josh Dibb, Noah Lennox)
This was the A-side and it is a reasonably faithful cover of the 2009 Animal Collective single 'My Girls', although the original is more restrained, almost introspective, always threatening to take off without doing so. The Tears For Fears version is a bolder arrangement that does not hold back.

It opens with a sample of a childlike voice that harks back to the band's debut album *The Hurting*, while sonically, it mines the same territory that Orzabal explored with his solo album. The vocals are cheery and beg the listener to join in. Orzabal sounds like he is in his element amongst all the studio trickery and there is a persistent keyboard rhythm that pulsates throughout the song. It's a bold and bright cover version.

'Ready to Start' (William Butler, Win Butler, Régine Chassagne, Jeremy Gara, Tim Kingsbury, Richard Reed Parry)

Where the Arcade Fire version starts with the sound of chiming guitars that then give way to a pounding bass and drum, the Tears For Fears cover is noticeably different. It starts with synth strings and a distinctive rhythm-centric backing. The opening almost sounds like a chamber orchestra, but the recognisable patterns from the original appear in flourishes as part of the keyboard pattern. This is a more drum&bass flavoured take of the Arcade Fire single from 2010, which can be found on their *The Suburbs* album. In fact, guitars are noticeably missing from the Tears For Fears version, apart from a burst after one of the choruses. Orzabal gets the lead vocal and the melody does share some similarities with Win Butler's original. Orzabal told *Rolling Stone* magazine how he constructed the song: 'I had that bloody melody going round and round and round in my head. It's not like the original.' He's right, but it sounds all the better for the song not being a carbon copy.

'And I Was a Boy from School' (Joe Goddard, Alexis Taylor)

Curt's presence is notably absent from the first two songs. Possibly because of the technology-heavy nature of the arrangements. His bass guitar is noticably absent throughout but he gets to contribute the vocals to the band's cover of the Hot Chip track from 2006. Unlike their cover of 'My Girls', they dial down their version a few notches compared to the original. It has a tender vocal from Smith, set against a skittering drum&bass backing. It's a minimalist cover version and one that fits the brief that Smith alluded to with his interview with *Stereogum*.

The Tipping Point

Personnel:
Curt Smith: Vocals, bass,
Roland Orzabal: Vocals, guitar, keyboards, rhythm programming
Charlton Pettus: guitars, keyboards, programming, mixing
Doug Petty: Accordion, Hammond organ, piano, string arrangement
Carina Round: backing vocals
Aaron Sterling: Drums
Jamie Wollam: Drums
Max von Ameln: Guitar
Jason Joseph: Vocal arrangement, choir
Charles Jones: Choir
Jessi Collins: Choir
Lauren Evans: Choir
Sacha Skarbek: Piano
Record label: Concord
Recorded: Roland Orzabal, Curt Smith, plus Sacha Skarbek, Florian Reutter
Release Date: 25th February 2022
Highest Chart Placings: UK: 2, US: 8,
Run Time: 42:25

Having said that *The Seeds of Love* had an epic gestation that was deserving of a book of its own, *The Tipping Point* would also deserve similar treatment.

In the time it took to write, record and release the album, the band experienced a number of challenges along the way. There were the usual management issues. That's a given for most bands with any longevity, but it has been especially true for Tears For Fears. Creative tensions between the original pair materialised once again, but instead of tearing the band apart, the pair reflected on what was going on and became closer as a result. The death of Roland Orzabal's wife, Caroline had a detrimental effect on Orzabal's health in this period too. There was also a global pandemic to contend with. The fact that there is an album at all is a testament to the pair's resilience.

The 2004 album 'Everybody Loves a Happy Ending' hinted at closure; the end of something. There may have been no new Tears For Fears songs in the last 18 years, but the band had not stopped performing. In that period, there was no ambition to write a new album, well, not at least until they had something to say. Curt Smith discussed the reasoning with *Forbes Magazine,* in 2022, about why they went back into the studio:

Initially, the premise of us doing a new record and why we felt that we wanted to do it, was we got to the point of playing live, which we do every year. It's thoroughly enjoyable because we love the band we have now. But we felt it would be great to have some new material because when you have a finite amount of material, there are only so many ways you can change the set. And so, I would say it was getting maybe a little boring for us.

The initial sessions for the album took the form of what the band likened to 'speed dating'. In these sessions, their management tried to bring Tears For Fears kicking and screaming into the modern world by getting them to work with the songwriters who were responsible for writing many of the hits of the day.

One of the band's 'speed dating' collaborations, 'I Love You but I'm Lost,' co-written with Dan Smith of Bastille, was released as the lead single to promote the 2017 compilation *Rule the World: The Greatest Hits*.

The new greatest hits album was designed to launch the next phase of the band, but once they handed over the tracks for the greatest hits (along with 'Stay'), they realised that the new album that they were working on was lacking something. It didn't feel like a Tears For Fears album. Smith detailed the tensions that were apparent in the initial stages of the album with Paul Sinclair in 2022.

We were doing this album, the 'broken album' as Roland calls it, and I didn't like it. In particular, I didn't think it had a narrative, a flow, and it was all very much one thing. And you get to that point where you ask yourself 'Can I really do this?'. So, I was at the point where I wasn't happy with it and Roland was actually quite liking it. Our manager liked it but wanted something *more* like that. And I was sort of stuck and no one was understanding where I was coming from.

A version of the album was ready for release just before the start of the coronavirus pandemic. 'The Tipping Point' single was first scheduled for April 2020, but the pair decided to go back to the drawing board and record some new songs. 'No Small Thing' and 'Rivers of Mercy' were the first fruits of these songwriting sessions. Orzabal and Smith came together with a couple of acoustic guitars and recorded the initial efforts on an iPhone. This gave the pair the impetus to finish the album and see the flaws in some of the other songs they had earmarked for the album.

One of the issues of the so-called 'broken album' was that the various producers used had their own idea of what Tears For Fears sounded like and they tried to replicate that, attempting to present the pair with facsimiles of their biggest hits.

Not all of the alliances were unsuccessful and one notable collaborator on *The Tipping Point* was Sacha Skarbek (who co-produces five songs and co-writes two). He had previously written songs for James Blunt, Miley Cyrus, and Duffy. Charlton Pettus, a long-time touring member of the band, has a hand in the production of seven songs, with co-writes on five, and was also responsible for most of the mixing.

After numerous delays, the album was finally ready in late 2020. Roland Orzabal reflected on the finished album with *HMV.com*, in 2022:

It was bizarre because I think by then, we'd had so many knockbacks and so many things that had undermined our confidence that you almost don't dare to say that something is great. I made comments to Curt like 'I think this could be a really good album' or 'I think we're going to get good reviews', and he'd just laugh. You would have thought someone like us would have all the confidence in the world, but no.

There are strong links between *The Tipping Point* and *The Hurting*. The band's official account tweeted that if the debut album was about 'the hurting', this one is about 'the healing'. Smith did say during Tim's Twitter Listening Party playback of the album that 'We wanted this album to have an overall feeling of redemption & optimism.'

Across the whole recording process, the band recorded over 30 tracks. Maybe some will see the light of day in the future, but for now, fans will have to be happy with the ten tracks (plus three bonus tracks on some releases) of *The Tipping Point*.

The album title represents many facets of the creation of the album. The song itself relates to the death of Orzabal's wife, but the narrative of the album looks at general 'tipping points'. Curt told the BBC in 2022:

We felt the world was very much at a tipping point. The rise of the right-wing, Trump being elected, the Black Lives Matter movement, the pandemic, the climate crisis… And I think, for us, going through this experience together was a tipping point personally because there were so many false starts. The fact that we did seemed like an apt title for us.

The production does take some getting used to at first, given the way that it has been mixed, it might not be for all tastes. It is noticeably loud, something that is evident with a lot of modern recordings. There are evident tweaks to the vocals at some points, Curt's in particular – that's not to suggest that he needed autotune: it's a sound that's somewhat in vogue. There are other mixes available that might be more to other people's tastes, the Steven Wilson Dolby Atmos and 5.1 surround sound mixes for instance.

The sonic textures are different from the last album which was written and produced more naturalistically, although that album was recorded 18 years ago and fashions have changed.

Smith and Orzabal have moved with the times, but they have done it in a way that is true to their principles. The true test of any song is how it is played live, 'The Tipping Point', 'Break the Man', 'No Small Thing', 'Long, Long, Long Time', 'My Demons', 'Rivers of Mercy' and 'End of Night' all made it to the setlist for the initial dates of the band's US and UK tour in 2022,

They all sounded great live and didn't seem out of place alongside the other songs in their back catalogue.

The album has been a commercial and critical success and it is a vindication of the time spent putting it together. Indeed, there has been universal praise for the album with the *Metacritic.com* rating at the time of going to press showing one middling review (from the UK newspaper *The Guardian*) and fourteen positive reviews from numerous press sources. The overall score for the album is 83%.

It is an album of elegance, grace and beauty. *The Tipping Point* is the sort of album that Tears For Fears should be making in 2022, and they have done so, eventually, on their terms. There are some contemplative elements and the subject matter is quite harrowing at times, but ultimately there is some optimism and joy. It is no clearer what defines a 'typical' Tears For Fears album, this has all the elements of their 80s and 90s records, but it is also very much of the here and now.

The cover is a beautiful Cinta Vidal painting. Both Curt and Roland saw the image independently of each other and realised that it would work well. They approached Cinta Vidal to see if they could include themselves in the image somehow, but she was busy finishing an exhibition, so they left it as it is. The various inserts come with several enigmatic images of the pair, looking noticeably older and, perhaps, wiser.

A meme that was posted around the time of the release suggests that images taken of the duo down the years make them look like a married couple who have had their photograph taken just after an argument. But one thing that has been heartening during the release of the album is that the connection between Orzabal and Smith seems better than ever and that augers well for their future.

'No Small Thing' (Roland Orzabal, Curt Smith)

The first song on the album opens with a delicately strummed acoustic guitar and it has echoes of both Bob Dylan and Johnny Cash. Curt came up with this folk/country riff and it was selected by the band as the opening track on the album because it sounds unlike anything they had done previously. The hope was that people would sit up and listen because of that. But by the time we get to the end of the song, the listener is in more familiar TFF sonic territory.

Even though the riff came from Curt, it also marks a return to one of Roland Orzabal's earliest influences; he told *The Quietus* in 2013:

I started playing the guitar, learned three chords and started writing songs. My first love, believe it or not, was country and western: Johnny Cash and a bit of Elvis.

Lyrically, it is another song that has a deeper meaning and it mines the trials and tribulations that the band went through to finish the album. It feels natural and less contrived, as if it's the antithesis of trying to write a song with hit songwriters. The song was written in early 2020, just before the pandemic took hold when the band went back to the drawing board. The pair got together with a couple of acoustic songs at Smith's home. Not only did it represent a restart, but also saw their songwriting return to the way it had been at the start of their career.

Orzabal told *The Creative Independent* website how the band arrived at this moment:

We had a crisis meeting, and [Smith] wasn't sure whether he wanted to carry on. So, I said, Okay, let's do this: I'll come around to your house with an acoustic guitar. We'll sit down, and we'll play around like we did when we were kids. I brought my iPhone to record it, and Curt started playing this riff and we were off. We had a song. I took it away back to England and then lockdown started, and the pandemic started. The Black Lives Matter protests, all these kinds of things. All of a sudden, we were in a completely different environment and the world, and we had a ton of things to sing about.

Curt Smith was quoted in the *NME* 2022 about his take on the song:

It's like that it could have been a song from the 70s or 60s acoustic folk album. The fact that we felt confident enough to go from there to the end of the song to where it's just absolute mayhem speaks to that sense of freedom, and that's our comfort zone musically.

After the initial sessions, Orzabal took it back to England to finish it but was not sure about the song. It was his new wife, Emily, who convinced him to send it to Curt, who loved the arrangement. They got together at the end of 2020 to finish it.

In the age of streaming, this song starts the journey, the overall narrative of the album. The band had joked about calling it 'Tears For Fears: The Musical', and it does feel like the record has a lot to say about the band. It's one of the few songs on the album where the guitars are in the foreground, with strong drums towards the end and the unforced nature of the song is clear to hear.

Even with all the studio embellishments, it is possible to imagine this stripped back to its essence of just guitars and vocals, although Orzabal has likened the big, Beatlesque climax to 'A Day in the Life' meets Led Zeppelin. 'It took us a long time to get those drums to sound like [the led Zeppelin song] 'When the Levee Breaks,' he said to *Tidal.com*, of the song's ending. It is one of the standout tracks and a great way to open the album.

'The Tipping Point' (Roland Orzabal, Curt Smith, Charlton Pettus)

This was the song that announced the band's comeback and it acts as the perfect distillation of how the band should sound today. In parts, it sounds like what has gone before, but with a contemporary feel. Opening with haunting electronica, it gets into its stride once the vocals kick in. This is unmistakably Tears For Fears, to the extent that he rhythm that underpins the song is reminiscent of their 80s hit 'Everybody Wants to Rule the World'.

The 'speed dating' songwriting sessions had not generally been well-received by the 'other' members of Tears For Fears, who had been around for so long that they felt they knew the band's DNA, as Roland Orzabal explained to Jill Riley at *The Current* in 2021.

Now I think Charlton [Pettus] was getting a bit miffed that we were working with other guys when he knew exactly – has been touring with us for years – he knew exactly how to write a Tears For Fears song. He thought, let me get some kind of moody synthesizer. Use the beat from 'Everybody Wants to Rule the World', a little of a 'Head over Heels' piano motif, and it sounds horrendous. It sounds like Frankenstein's monster. But in fact, what he created was the germ of the most beautiful, beautiful yearning song.

Despite the song's big pop sensibility, it is a poignant number and deals with Orzabal's anguish at watching his wife fade away. It was about wondering about the point his wife Caroline would make the crossover from life to death and about when the mourning would begin: 'Life is crazy and then it all turns to dust'. Orzabal and Smith share the lead vocals to express their mutual sadness at the loss of a person who was very dear to them and whom they'd both known since they were teenagers.

The video, directed by Matt Mahurin, whose previous credits include U2 and Metallica, is highly symbolic with its opening images of the withering flowers falling off the table and the ghostly presence of figures floating in and out of the shot. The pair convey heartfelt emotions within the song. It makes you wonder how they get through this one when they perform it live, given its difficult subject matter

'Long, Long, Long Time' (Roland Orzabal, Curt Smith, Charlton Pettus)

This is another track that feels very contemporary and again shows a growth in the band's sound. Orzabal took Smith and Pettus' experiment and made it more conventional. There is an electronic pulse that sits underneath the keyboard chords that drives the verses to a chorus that builds gradually.

Carina Round's contributions to the song should not be overlooked. To call it a backing vocal is understating what she brings to the song. Curt Smith's tender vocal sets the scene in the verses before he hands it over to Round, who delivers the chorus.

Lyrically, the song could be about Roland and Curt's relationship that had strained in the build-up to the album sessions 'we haven't been together in a long time', as confirmed by Curt, in an interview on the band's YouTube channel in 2022. Round and Smith's call and response vocal delivery on the chorus also suggest the song could also be about dealing with a romantic relationship.

'Break the Man' (Curt Smith, Charlton Pettus)

The third single to precede the release of the album is a Curt Smith and Charlton Pettus penned number that sees him take the lead vocals. The inspiration for the lyrics came from 2016 and Donald Trump's presidential campaign. He looked at the way that Trump had vilified Hillary Clinton, and as a father of two females, he feared for how things were shaping up in the US.

The song is a celebration of women and a call to end patriarchy in the wake of the #MeToo movement. 'The Man' is a reference to the masculine authority figure that counter-culturalists have railed against down the years. For Smith, the song is 'about a strong female – which is obvious, but it's really about breaking the patriarchy.' Thematically people have noted the similarities in the message between this song and that of the band's 1989 hit 'Woman in Chains'. Smith said to *GQ* in 2022, 'That was really about stopping the abuse of women, 'Break the Man' is actually about giving women more power'.

The song is up-tempo and opens with a delicate piano riff that initially suggests that it's going to be a slower-paced song. It's not. The bold guitar strums throughout the verses recall a similar style from the band's back catalogue – 'Pale Shelter' from their debut album. It's yet another acknowledgement of the band's past and there are more to come. This is set against a pulsing backbeat that drives the song along. It marries synthesizers and horn elements to good effect.

The video that accompanies the song is inspired by the lyrics and is in animation form. It is set in a grey anodyne world dominated by men who climb the structures, then panning to a larger and more colourful representation of what might be mother nature. Directed by WeAreMonkeys, with animation by Mihai Wilson and produced by Marcella Moser, the band don't appear in this one, but they state that the video 'encompasses a world that illustrates the constructed reality of the patriarchy'.

'My Demons' (Roland Orzabal, Florian Reutter, Sacha Skarbek)

This could have been written for Depeche Mode given its industrial electronic edge. They are a band that both Curt and Roland professed love for in the past. Orzabal told the *BBC* before the album's release: 'I do a pretty good vocal, but it was almost built for Dave Gahan.' 'My Demons' is the album's out-and-out banger; it is asking to be remixed by any of todays fashionable DJs.

Florian Reutter and Sacha Skarbek were one of the more productive partnerships in the years the band painstakingly put the album together. Unlike the other producers, the pair did not try to impose what they thought Tears For Fears should sound like and things worked more organically with this particular track. They recorded other songs together, 'Please Be Happy' was one, and the bonus release of 'Shame (Cry, Heaven)'. Others may materialise in some form down the line.

The song stemmed from a backing track that the producers had. The band liked what they heard and the melody came quickly after that. The band had a lot of fun in turning it into a Tears For Fears song, with Orzabal likened the lyrics to Paul Simon's "Boy in the Bubble' on acid', he said in an interview with the Sodajerker podcast. There are some engaging and interesting rhyming couplets throughout the song – it's one of Roland Orzabal's favourite lyrics on the album. The lyrical themes include electronic surveillance, control, 'us vs them', and gun violence. These are all heavy premises, but they are delivered in a tongue-in-cheek manner.

It mines similar territory sonically for Orzabal that he did on his *Tomcat's Screaming Outside* solo album, where he was guided more by the rhythm, and tone of the songs, than the lyrical themes. It is another shuffle, which the band have used to good effect down the years.

It was recorded initially in 2016, but when the band returned to the 'broken album' it was reworked with new lyrics and enhanced production. Sitting between 'Break the Man', 'Rivers of Mercy' and 'Please Be Happy' it does provide a tonal shift, but not one that is too jarring and it acts as a buffer between those thematically heavier numbers.

'Rivers of Mercy' (Roland Orzabal, Charlton Pettus, Doug Petty)

This is one of the standout tracks on an album that is brimming with highlights. It is such a strong song that it is comparable to many of the other highlights of the band's back catalogue. It's said to be Roland Orzabal's favourite track on the album.

It's a beautifully ethereal number that was written at a time of great contradictions. While Orzabal was at home in the English countryside, experiencing beautifully Mediterranean summer weather, the UK was experiencing its first lockdown during the Covid pandemic. When he turned on his television, he could see the unrest in the US in the wake of the George Floyd murder in June 2020. His killing at the hands of the police led to civil unrest in the US, as well as around the world.

This has the characteristics of a big gospel number in that it is a song that you could imagine a multi-harmony group would like to get their hands on to sing. Indeed, the song has the required amount of depth for such an arrangement. It also feels like they've written a standard for future generations; the sort of number that drips with empathy in the way that modern day talent show contestants love.

It was written after the band had regained a sense of direction and one of the instigators of the change was Orzabal's wife Emily, who said that Curt and Roland should record specifically with their touring band, which they did with great results. The backing track was written by Doug Petty and Pettus, who were working together on a film soundtrack and Orzabal used parts of that.

Orzabal said to *Variety Magazine* in 2022, that Doug Petty 'is sort of a dark-horse guy who hides his light under a bushel — kept his talent to himself. The guy is amazing'.

It's a soulful ballad taking its inspiration from the events of 2020. Where the song sits in the sequence of the album makes it all the more powerful. Beginning with just a chorus initially, the band managed to work it up into the finished track. The middle eight was the last piece of the puzzle. Petty and Pettus came up with the guitar arpeggio that recalls 'Women in Chains' – a nice easter egg for fans. 'There was a conflict between my reality in one part of the world with this desire for peace and the rage that was bubbling elsewhere. So that's where the song comes from. We start with some sounds from the riots and then we try and move away out of the rage,' Orzabal said to *Newsweek* in 2022.

Steven Wilson, a fan of the band and the mixer/producer of the band's 5.1 audio mixes, has dubbed 'Rivers of Mercy' 'as a future classic' in an email exchange with Orzabal. But 'Rivers of Mercy' also has that sophisticated pop sheen that recalls songs like 'Mercy Street' by Peter Gabriel and it is a beautiful way to start side two of the vinyl if that's the format that you are listening to the album on.

'Please Be Happy' (Roland Orzabal, Sacha Skarbek)

Probably the most poignant song on the album with its haunting, plaintive piano melody. It's a song that fans of the band would already be familiar with before it appeared on the album, as it had been available for a few years on YouTube with a solemn, black and white video. The original audio came from Roland Orzabal's Soundcloud account, which has Orzabal singing on that version, but it is Curt that takes the lead on this.

Lyrically it's an emotionally weighty song that deals with the illness of Orzabal's late wife. It was not originally in the reckoning to be on the album, as Orzabal didn't want to sing it for obvious reasons with Curt saying during the Tim Burgess Twitter Listening Party, in March 2022 that the segue from 'Rivers of Mercy' into this song breaks his heart. He was honoured when he was asked to sing this one, particularly as it was a difficult one for Orzabal to address during the recording sessions.

Producer Sacha Skarbek played some basic chords on the piano in the studio and captured the song on his iPhone. It is that version that has ended up on the album, with only minor modifications.

Orzabal's lyrics paint a picture of desperation and helplessness as he watches someone he loves struggling with depression. 'If you lay among the graves/you will see other ghosts'.

'Master Plan' (Roland Orzabal)

The theme of this song is familiar ground for the band, who, in their 40-plus years as musicians, they have experienced a few issues with the business side of the industry. There have been a few managers that have come and gone, who have not been aligned with the creative aspects of what the band is about. Songs like 'The Working Hour' and 'Cold' have covered various issues of this sort over the years.

In the period that it took to record the album, the initial idea for the band was not to record an album at all. This was something that their then-manager thought was not necessary as they were doing good sales numbers playing live as a 'heritage act'. The band were not even allowed to post wrk in progress online.

This is the song that rails against that attitude and thankfully, the band was determined to ignore this advice, along with the insistence, subsequently, that the band should write with younger, more fashionable acts. The result is 'Master Plan', which sits alongside this collection of songs that was a long time coming, but on the strength of the collection, it was well worth the wait.

Lyrically it's multi-layered. The song could be talking about a relationship, but it's actually about their ex-manager, Gary Gersh. It's the song that is the most Beatlesque on the album; there had to be at least one! It has elements of McCartney and ELO in its production, driven by a strident piano and equally driving percussion in the background. Curt Smith, on Tim Burgess' Twitter Listening Party, described the middle eight 'as bat shit crazy'. Indeed, it does reference The Beatles and The Rolling Stones in the lyrics, though this was almost omitted from the album, Curt said, in the same Twitter conversation.

There are yet more easter eggs in the song to keep the fans happy. You can hear Orzabal singing a line that sounds like 'Last Train to Norwich' at the end. This is a call back to something that was at the start of 'Schrödinger's Cat' a B-side of 'Break it Down Again'. Curt has said that this reference works because the song 'needed some light-heartedness and positivity at this point'.

'End of Night' (Roland Orzabal)

This is one of the oldest songs on the album and it underwent several remixes to get to *The Tipping Point* version. Curt was not a big fan of it initially but came around in the end. It's another song that, in the overall narrative of the album, works perfectly.

It appears to be a love song written by Orzabal for his new wife, especially when he sings about the 'mistral winds blowing in and making him happy again'. It's a song that has the big pop sensibilities that can be seen all over *Songs from the Big Chair* and came about with Orzabal coming up with different sounds on his laptop. The song did not change much from the original demo, on which it's a simple lead synth line. There's a lot of joy to be found here, acting as a counterbalance to some of the heavier themes – a simple pop song. It's the most up-tempo track on the album, with huge sweeping synth sounds and a swinging rhythm, as well as great harmonies from Orzabal and Smith.

'Stay' (Curt Smith, Charlton Pettus)

It's one of only two songs that does not have an Orzabal co-writing credit and it is a very personal number for Smith. It was originally intended for a solo project, but it has subsequently ended up on two Tears For Fears releases. The 'stay, don't go' conflict of the lyric was at a time when Smith was considering walking out on the band again. 'Go, don't go/Damned if I do, damned if I know'. These frustrations have managed to embolden the relationship between Curt and Roland instead of breaking the band apart, it also gave the band the impetus to get the album completed.

The song first appeared on the *Rule the World: The Greatest Hits* compilation album, released in 2017. On the compilation album, it felt like filler and didn't stand out amongst the other classics, so when it was announced that it would also appear on the new album, it was seen as a bit of disappointment, but in context, it fits perfectly. It is a superb song worthy of its place on *The Tipping Point*, linking thematically with a number of the others on the album, also having been remixed and mastered so that it fits in with the overall tone. Similar to 'Famous Last Words' it provides s a slow fade to the album.

Talking to Paul Sinclair at Super Deluxe Edition, Smith said of the song:

We were doing this album, the 'broken album' as Roland calls it, and I didn't like it. In particular, I didn't think it had a narrative, a flow, and it was all very much one thing. And you get to that point where you ask yourself 'Can I do this?' So, I was at the point where I wasn't happy with it and Roland was quite liking it. Our manager liked it but wanted something more like that. And I was sort of stuck and no one was understanding where I was coming from. If I had left, it would have been a painful decision, because Tears For Fears has been part of my life, and Roland has been part of my life, for a very long time. So, the song 'Stay' is really about that. It was a very sad time for me.

Extra Tracks (Super Deluxe Edition)

Super Deluxe Editions released a CD version of the album that included three extra tracks (see below). Given the long evolution of the album in the years preceding its release a super deluxe edition in the style of the packages that have been released for the band's first three albums may follow. There is an SDE-exclusive Blu-ray audio version of the album that does not contain extra tracks but does feature Steven Wilson's Dolby Atmos mix and his 5.1 mix of the album. That has been released in two editions. The first one is ultra-rare.

Bonus Tracks

The only 'singles' that accompanied the release were 'The Tipping Point', 'No Small Thing', 'Long, Long, Long Time' and 'Break the Man'. These were mainly for streaming and radio play and were not released in physical form, although they had accompanying videos. No extra tracks, B-sides or remixes have been released at the time of this book going to press.

'Secret Location' (Roland Orzabal, Curt Smith, Sacha Skarbek, Garret Lee)

This is one of the songs that emerged in the period of the band being told to look outside for different producers to get involved and it sounds very contemporary, not typically Tears For Fears, almost feeling like a pastiche of a modern pop hit. Like much of *The Tipping Point*, guitars are buried in the mix if they are on there at all, but there is a busy synth bassline. However, this track is a grower and it is unfortunate not to be on the standard edition of the album, available on YouTube for those without this edition.

'Let It All Evolve' (Roland Orzabal, Charlton Pettus, Curt Smith)

Of the three extra tracks, this is the strongest and the most like classic Tears For Fears, produced by the 'regular' songwriting team, and it could easily have fitted in on the band's previous album. The guitars are more prominent. There's an excellent bassline that kicks in during the second verse. The lyrics have a mantra-like quality to them, especially over the chorus, as the title is repeated.

'Shame (Cry Heaven)' (Roland Orzabal, Charlton Pettus, Florian Reutter, Sacha Skarbek, Curt Smith)

With the working title of 'The Shame', Curt Smith gets to sing this final extra track. It's a slow-building piano-driven song with a bassline that acts as the hook. This contemporary-sounding is the weakest of the three tracks, coming from a similar place sonically as 'Stay', which made the final cut for the album.

Official Compilation Albums

There have been three official compilations *Tears Roll Down (Greatest Hits 82–92)* (1992), *Saturnine Martial & Lunatic* (1996), and *Rule the World: The Greatest Hits* (2017). These collections were generally well-received by the fans as they offer a decent picture of the band's output at the points in the time that they were released.

Over the years, there have been several others that have been released on budget labels. These generally come out without being officially sanctioned by the band and these are generally best avoided given the scattergun nature with which they have been compiled, especially when the 2017 hits collection can be picked up in physical formats quite cheaply.

Tears Roll Down (Greatest Hits 82–92)

Release date: 2 March 1992
Label: Polygram (Phonogram/Mercury)
Highest chart places: UK: 2, US:53

With Curt leaving the band after the release of *The Seeds of Love* and a new album on the way, the time was right for a compilation to round-up phase one of the band.

The (original) 12-track album *Tears Roll Down (Greatest Hits 82–92)*, contains eleven of the band's singles, leaving out the charity single 'Everybody Wants to Run the World' and the much-maligned 'The Way We Are'. There is the addition of a new tune to give some value to those fans who have already purchased the band's back catalogue. The song in question is 'Laid So Low (Tears Roll Down)'.

The cover image for the album is a collage that has *The Seeds of Love* era sun symbolism in the foreground. Apart from the sun, the rest of the images seem to be quite random and do not seem to have a deeper meaning. There is no commentary or essay in the sleeve notes, their content just being the replication of the relevant song lyrics.

Only two singles were released as part of the campaign via the track that lends the collection its name 'Laid So Low (Tears Roll Down)', plus a further push for 'Woman in Chains'. This time it is credited as Tears For Fears featuring Oleta Adams. The front cover image replicated the mermaid image from the first release, but with the addition of a collage in keeping with the overall album design in the background. The single did not improve on the number 26 chart position of the 1989 release, charting at 57.

There is also a video collection called *Tears Roll Down (Greatest Hits 82–92)* which replicates the tracklisting of the album.

Tracklistings

1992 Original Release
'Sowing the Seeds of Love', 'Everybody Wants to Rule the World', 'Woman in Chains' (with Oleta Adams), 'Shout' (7' edit), 'Head Over Heels', 'Mad World',

'Pale Shelter', 'I Believe', 'Laid So Low (Tears Roll Down)' (Previously unreleased*),* 'Mothers Talk', 'Change' (7' Version), 'Advice for the Young at Heart'.

2004 Bonus Disc
The greatest hits package was reissued in 2004 as a 2-CD/1-DVD set as part of the Sound+Vision Deluxe brand. The extra disc contained the following tracks: 'Memories Fade', 'The Start of the Breakdown', 'The Hurting', 'The Marauders', 'The Working Hour', 'Shout' (US Remix), 'Standing on the Corner of the Third World', 'Johnny Panic & the Bible of Dreams', 'Break It Down Again', 'Elemental', 'Bloodletting Go', 'The Body Wah'.

2005 Bonus Remix Disc
There was a subsequent reissue with a bonus disc of remixes that has a variation in the cover design with the sun symbol more prominent. 'Shout' (Skylark 12' Extended Club Mix), 'Change' (Joey Negro Punkdisco Mix), 'Head Over Heels' (Dave Bascombe 7' N. Mix), 'Pale Shelter' (New Extended Version), 'Laid So Low (Tears Roll Down)' (US Dance Mix), 'Mothers Talk' (Beat of the Drum Mix), 'Sowing the Seeds of Love' (Wen's Overnight Mix), 'Shout' (Jakatta Thrilled-Out Mix), 'Woman in Chains' (Jakatta Awakened Mix Radio Edit), 'Mad World' (Afterlife Remix), 'Everybody Wants to Rule the World' (The Chosen Few Remix)

'Laid So Low (Tears Roll Down)' (Orzabal, Bascombe)
Highest chart places: UK: 17
The first song in the post-Smith era had its origins in a track that appeared on the B-side of the 'Sowing the Seeds of Love' single. The original B-side was a percussive Latin-style number with an extended instrumental and incantation that lead to the 'Tears Roll Down' chorus/outro. The new version is a more traditionally guitar-led number, with newly penned verses – mainly the 'laid so low' elements. There's a rockier guitar solo towards the end and whereas 'Tears Roll Down' is mostly instrumental and in 7/4 time, 'Laid So Low (Tears Roll Down)' has a chorus/verse structure and is mostly in 4/4 time. The updated lyrical element of the song was written after the split with Curt, and Orzabal has said that the phrase 'so low' is an intentional play on words (solo). The lyrics are also reflective of the deterioration of the relationship between the pair.
    The video opens with animated graphics, which run throughout the song. Orzabal can be seen in grainy sketch-like form. It's quite minimalist, and the song has barely been played live by the band down the years. It was not included on the *Rule the World: The Greatest Hits* album in 2017.

Saturnine Martial & Lunatic (B-sides and Rarities Compilation)
Record label: Polygram (Phonogram/Mercury)
Release date: 3rd June 1996

Highest chart places: Did not chart
Run Time: 78:32
Saturnine Martial & Lunatic rounds up the B-sides and other rarities from the band's Phonogram/Mercury years. While clearly a record company-planned release, it's good to have some of the deep cuts from the band on one collection, with some of the songs making it to CD for the first time.

Even though the tracks come from all parts of the band's history, it does feel like a coherent collection. There is a degree of authenticity about the release as it comes accompanied by sleeve notes written by Orzabal and erstwhile producer Chris Hughes, discussing the reasoning for some of the songs and the direction that the band took at the time of each release. The notes give insight into why some of the songs ended up as B-sides, though some deserved to be on full albums and in some cases, were even strong enough to be single releases. The collection acts as a forerunner to the deluxe editions.

The B-sides down the years have been a great place to find the band experimenting and at times often templating future material, while 'The Way You Are' finally finds a home on a compilation album.

Coming out after the release of the *Raoul and the Kings of Spain* album, there are no songs from that period. The title and the cover art are reflective of Orzabal's interest in astrology and the cover features astrological symbols representing Saturn, Mars and the moon. Orzabal is also credited with the sleeve design.

'Johnny Panic and the Bible of Dreams' (Roland Orzabal)
Highest chart places: UK: 70.
The title is borrowed from the name of a collection of short stories by the American writer Sylvia Plath. It features Biti Strauchn, a backing singer on *The Seeds of Love* tour, performing lines from 'Sowing the Seeds of Love' as a rap. There's a sample of Oleta Adams' voice in the mix too. It features an arpeggiated guitar part, over a drumbeat that appears to use the widely sampled James Brown, 'Funky Drummer' loop. There is a newly written lyric that covers the 'Johnny Panic' element of the song and in the album's sleeve notes, Roland Orzabal talked about the inspiration behind this version in the liner notes: 'At the time, I was curious to hear the verse of 'Sowing the Seeds' sung as a rap and it was this combined with a Talking Heads style chorus sung over the chord structure of 'Shout' that gave rise to the track.'

The original version of this song can be heard on the B-side of 'Advice for the Young at Heart'. It is also on the deluxe editions of *The Seeds of Love* box set that came out in 2020. The version that appears on this album is a longer remix by the DJs Fluke, which was remixed and anonymously released as a single in its own right in 1991, under the name Johnny Panic and the Bible of Dreams, although the Tears For Fears production and writing credits are visible on the sleeve of the release. The song got to number one on the British dance chart and number 70 on the UK's official singles charts. It's an inventive way to approach the remix of a song and as an experiment it worked out well.

'The Big Chair' (Roland Orzabal, Curt Smith, Ian Stanley, Chris Hughes)

The song was originally released as the B-side of 'Shout' and the title was the inspiration for the title of the band's second mega-selling album, *Songs from the Big Chair*. On the single release, the credit says 'under-produced by Ian Stanley,' no doubt self-deprecation, especially as the song is built around several simple samples. 'The Big Chair' in question, references the book *Sybil* by Flora Rheta Schreiber. The story is about a young girl who is psychologically traumatised and only recounts what happened to her in 'the big chair'. The book became a television film in 1976, starring Sally Field.

The song is built around several samples of the dialogue from the film, 'She wants to sit beside you in your big chair'. It's typical of the band's approach to B-sides in that era to produce something that was quite experimental. The keyboard sounds are similar to many used in film soundtracks at the time, especially Ryuichi Sakamoto. Writing in the sleeve notes for this album, producer Chris Hughes said: 'I always felt this piece was a soundtrack to the Middle Ages. Perhaps [Sybil]'s childhood horrors stemmed from those times; certainly, the Fairlight II we used to make it did.'

'Schrödinger's Cat' (Roland Orzabal, Alan Griffiths)

It's another Tears For Fears song that mines The Beatles' back catalogue for inspiration. There are other 60s references in the mix too. There's a dash of 'Sgt Pepper', a bit of 'I am the Walrus', again. There's also a piano break that obliquely recalls Thunderclap Newman's 'Something in the Air. In its finished form, it has single written all over it, but it missed the cut for the *Elemental* album because the was not finished in time.

The inspiration for the song stems from Roland Orzabal's interest in reading popular science books about quantum mechanics. The famous thought experiment of Erwin Schrödinger was used for the title. When interviewed by the physicist and science writer, Paul Halpern, in 2015, Orzabal said: 'Wonderful thought experiments such as Schrödinger's Cat have an almost poetic, visual quality to them, which, as a songwriter, I found inspirational, so much so that I managed to play with the concept in a song of the same name'.

'The last train to Norwich' shouted at various points, (although it can be mistaken as something about an orange), is another symbol for a clockwork universe. The clockwork universe theory compares the universe to a mechanical clock wound up by God. A perfect machine, with gears governed by the laws of physics. This is something that Orzabal discussed with Paul Halpern. This phrase is also referred to again on the 2022 album *The Tipping Point* song 'The Master Plan'. Roland Orzabal's novel published in 2014, *Sex, Drugs and Opera*, uses Schrödinger's Cat paradox as a plot device when a dog goes missing and the character finds himself in a state of hope and despair.

It's a hook-laden track and added great value as one of the B-sides/extra tracks for the 'Break it Down Again' single. It would certainly have been a worthy addition to the *Elemental* album, although it may have been one too many Beatles-inspired songs following so soon after 'Sowing the Seeds of Love'.

'My Life in the Suicide Ranks' (Roland Orzabal, Chris Hughes, Ian Stanley)

For a band that prides itself on its perfectionism with the recording process (often to the detriment of the schedule of releasing songs), this is the most underproduced release in its back catalogue. It came out of what was known as 'The Suicide Jam Sessions' and what was released was preserved from that time. The drum sample had been set up for 'Rhythm of Life'. Orzabal, Ian Stanley, Chris Hughes, and Dave Bascombe jammed around the idea. The song originally appeared as a B-side of the original 'Woman in Chains' single (it was omitted 1992 re-release). The sleeve notes state that it was recorded onto cassette, words, music, and everything created at the same moment. The song was inspired by a lull during the recording of *The Seeds of Love*. To this date, a more polished version has not been released, but the more decipherable lyrical elements have cropped up on 'Mr Pessimist' on the *Elemental* album.

'When in Love with a Blind Man' (Roland Orzabal, Ian Stanley)

This was a song that predated the *Songs from the Big Chair* era and stems from a motif that Ian Stanley came up with, with Roland Orzabal adding the melody line and the lyrics. It features Smith providing an ever so tender vocal performance and a synthesized shakuhachi flute, which was a feature of many a record in that period, Peter Gabriel, in particular, used it to good effect on his *So* album. It has a sparse piano line running through the song. The Fairlight was seemingly put to work on the synthesised strings, which are a feature of the song. Initially released as the B-side of 'Head Over Heels', the version here (and on the single) may be the original demo. The musical motif is identical to the one that runs through 'The Working Hour', as are some of the vocal melodies.

'Pharaohs' (Single Version) (Roland Orzabal, Curt Smith, Ian Stanley, Chris Hughes)

This was released as the B-side of 'Everybody Wants to Rule the World' The title 'Pharaohs' is a play on words of The Faroe Islands, which is referenced in the sample that runs throughout the song, taken from BBC Radio 4's shipping forecast. It is a gentle, calming piece in keeping with the broadcast it references. When all are in peril on the sea, the announcer will be calm and measured. The song provides a lovely counterpoint to the A-side and it shares some melodic similarities to that single, in that it incorporates the main melody and its guitar pattern but in a much slower form. The lightly emphasised drum beat is quite mellow too.

'Déjà-Vu and the Sins of Science' (Roland Orzabal, Alan Griffiths)

This comes from the *Elemental* era and it is one of the B-sides/extra tracks on the single 'Cold'. Conceptually the song comes from the same inspiration as 'Schrödinger's Cat', this time coming from an opposing perspective; it's an anti-science song. It has a mantra-like quality to it, especially with the repetition of the lyric: 'I must learn to protect myself/ I'm not a man of violence.' The song is peppered with samples of car doors slamming and even a Japanese monk, white noise and radio samples. The song has a strong bassline running alongside all the other sounds. It could be called 'a mess', but it makes for a more than passable extra track.

'The Marauders' (Roland Orzabal, Ian Stanley)

This has an oriental theme and Ryuichi Sakamoto seems again to be the inspiration. It is an instrumental track that was very much the work of Ian Stanley. No doubt from tinkering away at the Fairlight. It was the B-side of 'The Way You Are, and it is the more rewarding song from that release. It was a sign of the band continuing to experiment while still writing hit singles. Stanley's influence in this period should not be underplayed. Unusually for the band's more experimental songs, this one was in the live set at the same time that 'The Way You Are' was.

'Tears Roll Down' (Roland Orzabal, Ian Stanley)

Initially released in 1989 as the B-side to 'Sowing the Seeds of Love', 'Tears Roll Down' is a mostly Latin-influenced, mostly instrumental track. There is one section that contains the lyrics 'Where tears roll down' repeated four times. The song is mostly a 7/8 rhythm, a departure for the band when it was released. Like a few other songs from their back catalogue, it was later retooled in a more guitar-heavy version. With the additional verses and rejigged chorus, and big soloing middle eight, it was later renamed 'Laid So Low (Tears Roll Down)'. That was released as a single in 1992. Dave Bascombe is credited with a co-write on the update, but not Ian Stanley.

'New Star' (Roland Orzabal, Alan Griffiths)

Another song that could be filed under the 'too good for a B-side' category. It was in the running to be on the *Elemental* album, but it was another one that did not get finished in time. Given the delays in previous (and subsequent) album releases, it might have been a good opportunity to hold off releasing that album since there are several songs from that period that would have made great additions. It eventually ended up as the B-side for the 'Cold' single and has a great Orzabal vocal with guitars pushed to the fore. The intro is quite hooky too.

'The Body Wah' (Roland Orzabal, Alan Griffiths)

Another act of recycling is a slowed-down sample from the song 'Lord of Karma', later reused as part of the album track 'Elemental'. There is a sample of someone describing 'a well-known female politician' with the words, 'Because she has power, she has personality,' running through the song. It was another reference to Margaret Thatcher, the 'politician granny' referenced on 'Sowing the Seeds of Love'. This is quite a mellow track with a haunting keyboard line running through it and ghostly voices in the background. It was an extra track on the 'Laid So Low (Tears Roll Down)' single release.

'Lord of Karma' (Roland Orzabal, Alan Griffiths)
This is definitely in the 'try something out and if it doesn't work' stick it on the B-side category. Wordplay is evident throughout this playful song. There's a great guitar riff running through the song and Roland Orzabal said in the album's liner notes they were 'trying to get somewhere between the Happy Mondays and Jimi Hendrix's 'Crosstown Traffic''. It was originally an extra on the 'Laid So Low (Tears Roll Down)' single.

'Bloodletting Go' (Roland Orzabal, Alan Griffiths)
This was one of the first co-writes between Alan Griffiths and Roland Orzabal, feeling like it could have been written between *The Hurting* and *Songs from the Big Chair* albums. It's a return to the more electronic sound of the band's early days, but with the hindsight of several years experience. The partnership would write and record much of Orzabal's *Tomcats Screaming Outside* solo album – a collection of songs that would explore a similar sonic style to this. There are elements of Depeche Mode here, both musically and in the way that Orzabal delivers the vocals.

'Always in the Past' (Roland Orzabal, Ian Stanley)
Roland Orzabal can be heard saying 'do you know where I'm going?' at the start of the song, so it might offer some insight into the fraught nature of the recording process during that period. This B-side to 'Woman in Chains' has a memorable bass line and the sparseness of the production works in this setting, which is set against the typical way that the rest of the album at the time was recorded – one of Ian Stanley's last contributions, allowing him a co-write for composing the sax line produced on the Fairlight. As Orzabal says in the sleeve notes, 'the song was passed from Fairlight to Fairlight until it ended up in this shape, destined for the secret world of the B-side'.

'Sea Song' (Robert Wyatt)
A cover of the Robert Wyatt song from his solo album *Rock Bottom*. As Orzabal looked towards other influences while he was writing *Songs from the Big Chair,* producer Chris Hughes passed him a copy of the Wyatt album. 'Sea Song' became the B-side of 'I Believe (A Soulful Rerecording)'. In the *Classic Album* TV show, Hughes has remarked that while 'I Believe' was Orzabal's best Robert Wyatt impression at the time, he nails this one quite well too. This version sits nicely with the a-side and Robert Wyatt gets a dedication on the sleeve of the single.

'Ashes to Ashes' (David Bowie)

A fairly accurate interpretation of Bowie's hit. It was part of the *Ruby Trax* 40th anniversary collection for the *NME*. The band were given a list of number one songs by the music paper, which they didn't care for, so they eventually plumped for this classic. They tried to reinterpret the song originally, but instead, they came up with a perfect facsimile of the Bowie classic. The liner notes written by the *NME* on the original *Ruby Trax* album describe the version as 'suave'. They even self-reference their own 'Schrödinger's Cat' song in the mumbled part of the bridge, although the release of the *NME* album predates the release of that song.

'Empire Building' (Roland Orzabal, Curt Smith, Ian Stanley)

Another experimental B-side. It is a sample-laden track and complements the A-side 'Mother's Talk', totally in keeping with the band wanting to experiment. Orzabal admitted on the sleeve notes that he was 'listening to too much Art of Noise' (the British experimental instrumental ensemble) when this song was recorded. The song is constructed around a two-second sample of an early Simple Minds track 'Today I Died Again', which can be found on their album, *Empires and Dance*. This would be the second time that the Scottish band would be sampled by Tears For Fears, having previously used a sample of 'Waterfront' for 'Everybody wants to Rule the World'. The sample is quite repetitive and it is interspersed with samples taken from *Breaker Morant,* a film about the conduct of Australian soldiers during the Boer War.

'The Way You Are' (Manny Elias, Roland Orzabal, Curt Smith, Ian Stanley)

Highest chart places: UK: 24.
See *The Hurting* contemporary tracks.

Rule the World: The Greatest Hits

Release date: 10 November 2017
Label: Virgin EMI
Highest chart places: UK: 2
On the back of a series of live dates, *Rule the World: The Greatest Hits* was released. It was meant to kick start the campaign for the release of a new album soon. The band had initially signed a deal with Warner Brothers and a 12-track album was duly delivered but never released.

They bought themselves out of their Warner Brothers contact for the album and went to Universal, the label that had their back catalogue. Universal Music took two songs from the existing recordings, 'I Love You but I'm Lost' and 'Stay' and put out a greatest hits collection, the initial idea being that once the greatest hits came out, they would then release the new music. But no deal had not been done for the new album, so the label had no obligation to release it. What happened next is very much the story of how *The Tipping Point* was born.

The compilation has all the songs that you would expect from Tears For Fears. The notable omission is the 'Laid So Low (Tears Roll Down)' single, which lent its name to the band's first compilation. There is still no place for 'The Way You Are' or 'Everybody Wants to Run the World.' The 'Ready Boys & Girls' covers are not featured either. However, the collection does include the singles 'Break it Down Again' and 'Raoul and the Kings of Spain' from the time that Curt Smith was absent. 'Closest Thing to Heaven' from the reunion album *Everybody Loves a Happy Ending*, is included, as well as the two new songs. It is notable that 'Woman in Chains' is again credited as Tears For Fears & Oleta Adams.

The front cover has a collage of images that have some relevance to the band's back catalogue. The world is served up by a tiddly attired butler who serves up the world on a silver platter. The sunflowers and sun symbolism is used again to good effect. The sleeve notes on the vinyl and booklet of the CD version are so scant, that they are almost non-existent and there are no lyrics, only production and writing credits, alongside contemporaneous images of Roland and Curt.

Tracklisting: 'Everybody Wants to Rule the World', 'Shout' (7' edit), 'I Love You but I'm Lost', 'Mad World', 'Sowing the Seeds of Love', 'Advice for the Young at Heart', 'Head Over Heels', 'Woman in Chains' (with Oleta Adams), 'Change' (Single Version), 'Stay' (Previously unreleased), 'Pale Shelter' (2nd Single Version), 'Mothers Talk' (U.S. Remix), 'Break It Down Again', 'I Believe', 'Raoul and the Kings of Spain', 'Closest Thing to Heaven' .

'I Love You, But I'm Lost' (Roland Orzabal, Curt Smith, Mark Crew, Dan Smith)

New tracks on compilation albums are sometimes seen as filler, but given the wait between albums for fans of Tears For Fears, the two new tracks that appeared here were a big deal. Firstly, it was a chance to gauge how a new album could potentially sound and also, it was a chance to listen to the first new material from the band in over a decade.

The first of the new songs that the band had written from the sessions for what the band have dubbed the 'broken album', is one that they wrote during the round of sessions with many contemporary songwriters, with the mission to write a hit. In this instance, it was with Mark Crew, producer and Dan Smith, the lead singer of the band Bastille. Sonically it has a more electronic edge to it – a very contemporary sounding number. There is a big chorus with a sample that acts as the hook.

Roland Orzabal, when talking *to Classic Pop* in December 2017, said that the song 'is a love song but really about a lack of commitment. It's something that a man should never say to a woman and vice versa'. That this was a song that Roland liked but Curt didn't care much for demonstrated that past tensions had not entirely disappeared.

'Stay' (Curt Smith, Charlton Pettus)

Released initially as a bonus track on this compilation this song would eventually find its way to *The Tipping Point* in a remixed form. At the time, it felt like passable filler, feeling out of place sitting between 'Change' and 'Pale Shelter' in the running order. The song itself was one that Curt wrote and then sending it to Roland Orzabal and he put more rhythm parts on it, taking it to another level. The theme of 'Stay' is the time when Curt Smith was questioning whether he wanted to stay in the band around this time.

Curt Smith Solo

Soul on Board

Personnel:
Curt Smith: vocals & bass
Jeff Bova: keyboards
Kim Bullard: keyboards
Peter Cox: backing vocals
Paulinho Da Costa: percussion`
Kevin Deane: keyboards & producer
Lynn Davis: backing vocals
Steve Ferrone: drums
Siedah Garrett: backing vocals
Franne Golde: backing vocals
Taz i.e. No Fisk: Rap
Billy Livsey: keyboards & backing vocals
Jean McClain: backing vocals
Martin Page: bass, engineer, keyboards, producer, & backing vocals
Richard Sortomme: strings
Neil Taylor: guitar & backing vocals
Colin Woore: guitar
Record label: Phonogram/Mercury
Recorded: Curt Smith, Martin Page, Chris Kimsey, & Kevin Deane
UK Release Date: August 23 1993
Highest Chart Placings: UK: DNC.
Run Time: 51:42

In the same year – 1993 – that Roland Orzabal revealed his hand as to the direction of Tears For Fears, his erstwhile partner Curt Smith released his debut solo album. As part of the settlement of the band's split, Orzabal kept the name and Smith got an Audi Quattro car, amongst other things. Following the acrimonious split, Smith moved to the US and the 90s was a good period for him. He had not enjoyed being in the public eye, his marriage to Lynn had ended and he grasped the chance to get out of the spotlight.

He was still under contract with Phonogram/Mercury and he set about recording the album. Curt has discussed over the years that there may have been some 'contractual obligation' aspects to the creation of it and while there are some good moments, they are few and far between.

In the UK, the album release was preceded by the single 'Calling Out'. Both were ultimately unsuccessful and failed to chart. A second single, 'Words', also failed to make any impact. This failure saw the US release being shelved, despite promotional copies being issued.

But there are some notable Tears For Fears alumnae on the album. Nicky Holland co-wrote the single, 'Words', while Neil Taylor, Tears For Fears' live guitarist plays on a few tracks and co-wrote a B-side.

The main issue is that the album seems out of step with the music of its time. The list of credits highlights a lack of coherence to the tone and the approach to the songs. There are many co-writes, which all make it a fairly unremarkable album that has not aged particularly well. It has not made it to streaming platforms and it's hard to find these days, not even available on Curt's Bandcamp page.

The front cover has a moody image of Smith shot with a brownish sepia tint.

'Soul on Board' (Curt Smith, Martin Page)

The opening title track sets the tone of what was to follow in terms of production and style, suggesting that this is going to be a very mainstream album – ironic, given the limited success it had. A fretless bass rumbles along in the background, which dated the sound even when it was released. The drums sound a little dated and they are at times distracting. That said, Curt's vocals are tender as ever on a song about new beginnings. The lyrics seem heartfelt, but the song is unremarkable.

'Calling Out' (Curt Smith, Franne Golde)

Highest chart places: UK: DNC

Two songs in and it is clear that we are in 'white soul' territory. The lead single has all the tropes of that style and the soulful backing singers and another earnest vocal performance from Smith offer a slick and MTV-friendly sound. The video is aimed at that market too and like the rest of the album, it is elaborately produced.

Lyrically, he is calling out for God. It's about someone who is having a moment of uncertainty and is looking for a positive sign. The album cut is a fairly lengthy tune at (6:07), although the single release is shorter at (4:17). An 'unplugged mix' appeared on the single without offering anything different to the standard version.

'Beautiful to Me' (Curt Smith, Scott Wilk)

This is a pleasant enough tune and the way the piano and the guitar work together at the start almost sounds like the Scottish band Deacon Blue's 'Dignity'. It's a love song, the subject no doubt being Frances Pennington – his then partner and eventually his wife. Otherwise, it's an inoffensive album track. The song also appears on the 'Words' single with a different mix that emphasises the vocals.

'Wonder Child' (Curt Smith, Billy Livsey)

It's one of the better songs on the album and it has held up well. It has a strong melody and chorus and it is one of the few songs where the guitars are quite prominent in the mix. It's another track that seems to be addressing the feeling of being lost and the wonder child in question seems to be Curt. The lyrics do seem to be quite introspective.

'Words' (Curt Smith, Nicky Holland)
Highest chart places: UK: DNC
The second non-charting single from the album and it's a co-write with Nicky
Holland. It's an upbeat number, but as a single release in 1994, it feels out of
its time. There is a bit of wah-wah guitar plus a guitar solo in the middle eight
that dates the song even more.

'I Will Be There' (Curt Smith, Martin Page)
The years have not been kind to this song. It's a love song and it feels like filler.
The dated and formulaic sound that occurs throughout the album is again ever
present. Smith's vocals get lost in the heavy production.

'No One Knows Your Name' (Curt Smith, Colin Woore)
This song opens with a guitar backing before a plaintive Smith vocal kicks
in. The guitars during the intro have an American college rock feel to them.
The rock guitar cliches are employed to the full and this does shift the overall
sombre tone of the song a little.

'Rain' (Curt Smith, Billy Livsey)
A big MOR rocker that covers similar musical and lyrical ground to much of the
rest of the album. It's one to skip.

'Come the Revolution' (Curt Smith, Martin Page)
This is something of a change, and probably the most overtly political moment
on the album, but it feels a bit contrived and tokenistic, especially with the
rap from Taz i.e. No Fisk. It is the one song on the album that nods to the
contemporary sounds of the time, albeit in a watered-down and overproduced
way. Peter Cox, from British band Go West, guests as a backing vocalist.

'Still in Love with You' (Phil Lynott)
A cover version of the Thin Lizzy song from 1974 and It's a fairly faithful
rendition - a decent version of the song. There is another acoustic version of
the song on the 'Words' single that's worth checking out. That one is stripped
to the bone. There is a delicately strummed guitar with occasional flourishes
of slide that can be found on the album version. The arrangement of that is so
sparse that at times it almost feels like an acapella rendition.

Stand Alone Singles, B-sides, EPs and Other Contemporary Tracks
'Deal' (Neil Taylor, Billy Livsey, Jim Copley)
This is written by two veterans of the Tears For Fears touring band, guitarist
Neil Taylor and drummer Jim Copley. One of the B-sides/extra tracks on the
'Calling Out' single, it's an instantly forgettable tune. The guitars have that

MOR style and there is an extended guitar fill at the end that would not have sounded out of place on a song by Canadian rock singer Bryan Adams.

'How Does it Feel' (P Crowther, Neil Taylor)
The other extra track on 'Calling Out' is lacking in any noticeable hooks. Another short and instantly forgettable song.

Mayfield
Personnel:
Curt Smith: vocals & bass guitar
Charlton Pettus: guitar & backing vocals
Doug Petty: keyboards
Russ Irwin: keyboards & backing vocals
Shawn Pelton: drums
Steve Ferrone: drums
Brian Geltner: drums
Jimmy Copley: drums
Richard Pagano: drums
Carol Steele: percussion
Bob Muller: percussion
Tim Beatty: harmonica
Chris Rael: backing vocals
Rebecca Martin: backing vocals
Georg Brandi: accordion
'The Irish guy whose name we've forgotten': whistle
'The trumpet player from 'Cats': trumpet
Janice Whaley: backing vocals, 'instruments,' and arrangement
Record label: Zerodisc
Recorded: Charlton Pettus & Curt Smith
UK Release Date: 1998 (Rereleased 15 November 2011)
Highest Chart Placings: DNC
Run Time: 45:28

Following the failure of the first album, Curt Smith retreated from the music business and little was heard from him in terms of new music. He had moved to New York and the anonymity it brought him was a relief. But it was also a time that reinvigorated his love for music. At first, he had a syndicated college radio show and he also had a stint as a VJ on MTV. That was a bit more corporate and did not bring the same satisfaction as the college radio job.

In the mid-1990s, he met Charlton Pettus in New York. Smith said to *Stereogum* in 2022:

> He dragged me sort of kicking and screaming into his apartment to write songs. I say that facetiously, but it wasn't something I was thinking of. He was

116

like, 'What are you doing? You should be writing; you should be singing. By the end of the '80s, that had been kicked out of me, because it had just become a business. I'd lost that passion for it. That's what New York gave me back, between the radio show and forming a band under the radar. It's what I was missing at the end of my initial time in Tears For Fears.

He said in the sleeve notes he intended to 'try to rediscover the joys of music through playing live. He wanted to do it with a degree of anonymity, hence the band name Mayfield – Curt is Mayfield (referring to soul star Curtis Mayfield) was the inspiration for the name. The reconnection with the music came with him playing in downtown New York clubs such as Brownie's, Mercury Lounge and CBGB's, all within walking distance of his apartment on Mercer and Houston. This approach to gigging revitalised him as a musician and songwriter and the 'Mayfield Walking Tour' was born.
Curt Smith has said about the album on his Bandcamp page:

These were probably a couple of the most enjoyable years I've spent as a musician: no pressure and just doing it for the love of music. These songs were ostensibly recorded live, that is with the band playing together with overdubbing and editing used only to polish a few things. We recorded them over three weeks, and whilst I may question the quality of some of the recordings and mix in retrospect, I still can feel the passion intended today.

The main issue with his previous solo album was mainly one of identity. No one wanted an album that was Tears for Fear-lite, but it was hard to say what the album was supposed to be. But this album does feel like it represents a style that is true to Curt Smith.
The *Mayfield* album began as ten tracks for the 1998 release, but as the company that distributed the album was no longer in existence, the 2011 re-release came out on Smith's label with an extra track, a re-recorded version of 'Trees' with Janice Whaley.
This is the strongest of the Curt Smith solo albums and he can be forgiven for the Mayfield pun. There is very much a style and a tone evident in what he is writing, but little did we know that this was the start of Tears For Fears Mark III as the album includes Charlton Pettus and Doug Petty, two key members of Tears For Fears in its twenty-first-century form. Smith and Pettus have formed something of a productive songwriting partnership down the years.
Even though this was released under the name of Mayfield, it feels very much like the first true Curt Smith album. It is true to the sound that he would develop on subsequent solo releases and on some of the songs that he was to write for Tears For Fears, often in collaboration with Pettus. It has clear that meeting Pettus has had a positive effect on his songwriting style.
The front cover image of the original CD release has four pictures of Curt Smith in his 'bleached blonde' phase. They are set against a backdrop of four

colours (white, yellow, light blue and brown). The subsequent digital re-release has a solitary image of Smith set against a yellow background.

'What Are We Fighting For?' (Curt Smith, Charlton Pettus)
This is the perfect opener for the album with a few Tears For Fears elements in there, in particular the guitars and the brass at the end, plus a distinctive Pettus guitar solo of the type that would soon become familiar. All in all, it's a great opener. This would also end up as one of two bonus tracks on a future Tears For Fears release, the *Secret World Live in Paris* album.

'Sorry Town' (Curt Smith, Charlton Pettus)
Two songs in and the *Mayfield* album already has the coherence that was sadly lacking from *Soul on Board*. The theme seems to be that Smith is doing fine while others around are not, while musically this one is quite the rocker. The band that Curt Smith has surrounded himself with is a really solid and coherent unit and that comes through with this song in particular.

'Jasmine's Taste' (Curt Smith, Charlton Pettus)
After a brisk opening, the third track is a more laid-back number. The trademark warm and tender Smith vocal is put to good effect and there is a minimalist backing in the verses. A lightly picked guitar complements the vocals before the song ramps up for the chorus. It's one of the longer tracks on the album, but its strong melody earns it the right to be as long as it wants.

'Reach Out' (Curt Smith, Charlton Pettus)
Opening with an acoustic guitar and bass, this song has a distinctly country feel to it. The middle eight is the rockier element of the song before returning to a more brooding verse and chorus – more Nashville, than New York. The lyrics might be the aftermath of an argument, while the 'reaching out' in the last line of the song is less ambiguous, with Smith begging someone to 'go forth', but in somewhat stronger terms.

'Trees' (Curt Smith, Charlton Pettus)
This is a more contemplative number. It opens with light percussion and a more understated tone throughout. There is a drone-like melody that underpins the song, the vocals are in harmony with the meditative quality of the backing. The lyrics are very elemental, finding Smith at one with nature, perhaps reflective of England.

'Mother England' (Curt Smith, Charlton Pettus)
Another song that uses his former homeland as inspiration and it is one of the most overtly political songs on the album. This political consciousness has become more noticeable in Smith's later work and although the song

was written in the 1990s, it could almost be an anthem for the UK at a time that it went through the Brexit vote. The song eschews the concept of overt patriotism and not 'believing in imaginary lines. It has a singalong quality to it and it feels like it may be in the wrong place on the album as it feels like an album closer, especially given the epic nature of the music. The longest cut, it's also an album highlight.

'Snow Hill' (Curt Smith, Charlton Pettus)
This is another contemplative song as Smith again thinks of home, this time with a more nostalgic view of the place where he grew up. The beautiful and dreamy song is at odds with his home environment. While Bath is one of the most beautiful places in the UK, like a lot of places, it's not all picture postcard beauty. Snow Hill was certainly one of those places when Curt lived there. There is a lullaby quality to the song, while the minimalist piano and vocal arrangement serve it well. A middle-eight break drifts off in a reverie before the song returns to its chorus. There is a wonderfully heartfelt vocal – it's a tender paean to the place Curt grew up in. The song was released in May 2000 as a charity single for the London Road Carnival, in Bath. The release was limited to the Bath area, with only a small number of copies in circulation. The song was performed live several times in 2004 when Tears for Fear toured to promote their *Everybody Loves a Happy Ending Album*.

'I Don't Want To Be Around' (Curt Smith, Charlton Pettus)
It's another mellow track. It has a lazy, hazy feel to it. Sounding like it was a song written about the day after the night before, lyrics are almost a stream of consciousness. It's another slow-building song which fits in well with the overall tone of the album. One of the criticisms of *Soul On Board* was that it lacked cohesion and it didn't know what it wanted to do from a musical perspective. Having a band gives this album a focus that was sadly lacking and while this song might wash over the listener somewhat, it does sit in well as part of the album.

'Sun King' (Curt Smith, Charlton Pettus)
So far, the songs from Smith's solo era songs had not addressed the split from Tears For Fears and in particular Roland Orzabal. Perhaps some did subtly, but this song has no ambiguity. Tears For Fears fans may have read into the lyrics of 'What Are We Fighting For?' as a chance reunification, but listening to this song, the repairing of that relationship seemed unlikely to happen. It is a response to Roland's assessment of Smith from his song 'Fish Out of Water' (from the *Elemental* album). It starts in a mellow fashion, but the rage explodes after the first verse. The references to the elements and all things planetary can't hide that this is a dig at Orzabal, but of the two 'diss tracks', ('Fish out of Water'), this is the better one from a musical point of view. It opens with a Hammond organ before Smith's vocals kick in. The guitars come crashing in over the

chorus, which features the lines 'You make the earth revolve/ You make the camera sing/ No conscience can absolve/ The Sun King'. There is a certain level of anger in the way the guitars are treated.

'Gone Again' (Curt Smith, Charlton Pettus)
A gentle end to the record. This is a guitar and vocal number with some keyboard embellishments. It's a mournful closer, perhaps written from a female perspective. The person that has 'gone again' is yearning for that lost partner.

Extra track on the 2011 edition
'Trees' (feat. Janice Whaley) (Curt Smith, Charlton Pettus)
The re-released album came with an extra track featuring a duet with Janice Whaley. It's an update of the version of the song that appeared on the original release. It still has a meditative feel to it, but the song is given a more contemporary sheen with the electronic bedding in the background. Curt still takes the lead vocals, but the additional female vocals complement the song. Despite all the embellishments, it still has a calming and elemental tone.

Aeroplane
Personnel:
Curt Smith: vocals, backing vocals, bass, & guitar
Charlton Pettus: keyboards, guitars, & backing vocals
Dan Petty: guitars, keyboards, & backing vocals
Jack Petruzzelli: guitars & keyboards
Rob Arthur: guitars & keyboards
Doug Petty: keyboards & backing vocals
Richard Pagano: drums & percussions
Record label: Sour Music
Recorded: Curt Smith
UK Release Date: (Canadian Release: 1999) (US Release: 2000)
Highest Chart Placings: DNC

This is where Curt Smith's discography gets a bit confusing. The third album was also released as an EP, with the same name in some territories. The Canadian version is a full album of tracks that has songs from various parts of his previous and future releases, while the US EP release was a taster of the next solo album. It was also a good chance to record reworked versions of Tears For Fears songs 'Pale Shelter' and 'Everybody Wants to Rule the World'. The cover image is quite literal in that it is a black and white composite picture of an aeroplane on a runway.

Canadian Release (1999)
Tracklisting: 'Aeroplane', 'What Are We Fighting For', 'Sorry Town', 'Jasmine'

(previously known as 'Jasmine's Taste'), 'Reach Out',

'Pale Shelter' (Roland Orzabal)

This is a solo take on *The Hurting* classic. The opening guitar lick has a Madchester (1990s indie rock from Manchester, UK) vibe about it.

'Trees', 'Where Do I Go', 'Mother England', 'Snow Hill', 'I Don't Want to Be Around', 'Sun King', 'Gone Again'

'Everybody Wants to Rule the World' (Acoustic) (Chris Hughes, Roland Orzabal, Ian Stanley)

It's a really good acoustic take on the band's biggest hit. It has a nice picked guitar pattern all the way through and the keyboard arrangement takes care of the part that ramps up on the original. The solo sounds great, even when played on an acoustic guitar.

(Hidden Track) 'Snow Hill'

US EP version (2002)

'Aeroplane', 'Pale Shelter', 'Where Do I Go', 'Snow Hill', 'Reach Out', 'Everybody Wants to Rule the World'

Halfway, Pleased (2007)

Personnel:
Curt Smith: vocals/bass guitar
Charlton Pettus: backing vocals/guitar
Fred Eltringham: drums
Doug Petty: keyboards
Roland Orzabal: keyboards
Wendy Page: backing vocals
Sophie Saillet: backing vocals
Record label: XIII BIS Records
Recorded: (2001- 2008)
UK Release Date: 20th May 2008
Run Time: 67:00

The third solo album continues the tone that he established on *Mayfield*. This release came three years after the Tears For Fears comeback album and Smith was content at this time to balance his solo work with the day job. The album sessions had started at the turn of the century but were put on hold while Smith concentrated on the *Everybody Loves a Happy Ending* album. It wasn't until 2006 that the sessions concluded and it was initially released in France, in 2007.

Curt Smith dropped the Mayfield band name as it was deemed to be unhelpful in terms of marketing and cataloguing, but he carried on working with the same band line-up and songwriting team that had been instrumental with the last album. By this point, Curt's solo band had now been incorporated into the Tears For Fears line up too.

In terms of solo material, Smith has been more prolific than his Tears For Fears partner and It's an album that suggests that Smith had found his 'solo' voice. It was now a lot easier to define what was a Curt Smith record. However, the album did feature one notable guest appearance, none other than Roland Orzabal on keyboards. The front cover artwork features Curt, walking away; his back to the camera with his two daughters. The picture is framed to look like something that most families would have on their mantlepiece or shelf at home.

'Perfect Day' (Curt Smith, Charlton Pettus)
This is a calming opener to the album,in that mellow reflective style befitting a Curt Smith album. The opening lyric references Elvis, but the rest of the song is more influenced by another aspect of the American music scene with very Beach Boys-esque vocals. It has a beautiful summery vibe that sits well with the rest of the album. It's a gentle and pleasant opening to the album.

'Seven Sundays' (Chesney Hawkes, Charlton Pettus)
With a light keyboard with programmed drum beats back, this is a slow-building song with a melodic chorus. A chiming, catchy melody runs through the song. It's credited as a co-write between Chesney Hawkes and Charlton Pettus. Hawkes had a number one hit in the UK in 1991 with the song 'The One and Only'. The original version of this song appears on Hawkes' US album *The One and Only*. The Pettus/Hawkes collaboration has seen the pair work on a musical called 'The One' in recent years – tracks from the pair were posted on YouTube in 2021. An acoustic version of the 'Seven Sundays' is also available as a bonus track.

'Halfway pleased' (Curt Smith, Charlton Pettus)
The title track of the album starts with a sample of a young child. It has an electronic pulse underscoring the melody, while a sparse, hypnotic piano line serves to act as the element that holds it all together. The vocal is understated, but it is tender while the vibrating sounds ramp up towards the end as the guitars emerge. It's a trip-hop-influenced number.

'Greatest Divide' (Curt Smith, Charlton Pettus)
This is another mellow tune with a trip-hop-influenced backbeat, allied with a great bassline. This is set against elegantly strummed acoustic guitars. The slide guitar at the end is sublime and adds to the laid-back nature of the song. There is a great melody and it's one of the highlights of the album.

'Coming Out' (Curt Smith, Charlton Pettus)

This is one of several contemporary reference points on the album. The keyboard line is what drives the song initially before the beats kick in on a minimalist song. An acoustic guitar-led version is also available as a bonus track.

'Aeroplane' (Curt Smith, Charlton Pettus)

This is a song that lent itself to the title of the more abbreviated Canadian released LP and US EP. This is another mellow and meditative song with Curt using the soft register that he employs so well across the album. Lyrically it seems to be about flight – about being somewhere else. The bassline is quite arresting, and the vocals are tender. The backing is quite in keeping with the rest of the album. There's also a big middle eight that takes off in a different direction. It's very 1970s in tone.

'Two' (Curt Smith, Charlton Pettus)

The song opens with a melody that could almost be from a film score. The vocals and a keyboard are to the fore throughout once the filmic background fades away. It's another slow-building song. There are great vocal harmonies throughout. Smith has talked about his love of albums that have an overarching narrative and it is clear that there is one with this album. It demands to be played and listened to as a whole and does not lend itself to being filtered out, playlisted and segmented like most songs do these days.

'Addict' (Curt Smith, Charlton Pettus)

The mantralike quality of the song is good, with a pulse that runs under it. There is a faint sample so what sounds like someone being told to breathe. There are elements of Pink Floyd at their most atmospheric, especially as the guitars spiral away towards the end.

'Cover Us' (Curt Smith, Charlton Pettus)

This is a delicate acoustic number that has a fingerpicked guitar under a soft Curt Smith vocal. It's a nice interlude, with a folky vibe.

'Who You Are' (Curt Smith, Charlton Pettus)

This song appeared on *Everybody Loves a Happy Ending*, although the version here has a sparser arrangement. It begins almost a capella in style, before the drum beat and keyboard arrangements kick in and the song ramps up with wah-wah guitar and a great bass line. The middle eight breaks down into a psychedelic sonic assault, but the vocals offer a tender contrast.

'Where Do I Go' (Curt Smith, Charlton Pettus)

There's a bit of backwards guitar at the start that suggests the song might be about to become an out-and-out rocker. But it's not; it's another smooth number with piano and vocals at the heart of it and some ambient noises in the background. Its descending chord structure is very Beatlesque and there's a great guitar line to close.

Bonus tracks
'Snow Hill' (Live) (Curt Smith, Charlton Pettus)
A live cut of the *Mayfield* release. This is a beautiful piano and vocal arrangement of the song.

'Seven Sundays' (Duet with SO) (Curt Smith, Chesney Hawkes, Charlton Pettus, Sophie Saillet)
This is another version of the song. This time it's a duet with the French singer Sophie Saillet.

Deceptively Heavy
Personnel:
Curt Smith: vocals,
Charlton Pettus: backing vocals, guitars, keyboards, drums
Aaron Sterling: drums
Doug Petty: keyboards
Zoe Keating: cello & cello arrangements
Carina Round: lead & backing vocals
Holly Palmer: backing vocals
Claire Acey: backing vocals
Georgica Pettus: backing vocals
Harry Pettus: backing vocals
Michael Wainwright: backing vocals
Record label: Kook Media
Recorded: Charlton Pettus & Curt Smith
UK Release Date: 15th July 2013
Highest Chart Placings: DNC
Run Time: 48:01

Deceptively Heavy, is the fourth solo album (of new tunes), and his first in five years. It came out via Amazon.com and it is one of the rarest of his releases in physical form – limited to 500 copies on CD. It was released just before Tears For Fears entered the studio for the first time to start work on the new album, although, in the end, it is more likely that they recorded the *Ready Boys & Girls EP*.

The album cover has a mannequin of a figure dressed in a grey Ben Sherman T-shirt, a favourite Curt Smith brand.

'Beautiful Failure' (Curt Smith, Charlton Pettus)
Befitting a song written for Smith's eldest daughter, the album opens with a beautifully tender song written for his then-ten-year-old. She was going

through a period of self-doubt and the title came from her perceptions of herself, not how her father saw her. With a beautifully thoughtful chorus, it is a reassuring conversation piece between father and daughter.

'Suffer the Silence' (Curt Smith, Charlton Pettus)

A brittle piano and sparse backbeat introduce this song which seems to be aimed at someone who has been interfering in Curt's business. The sleeve notes mysteriously suggest that there has been 'temptation'. It is a call to people to stay out of his affairs; a pointed but nicely articulated rebuke.

'Hold It Together' (Curt Smith, Charlton Pettus)

This song was originally written for an indie movie called *Meth Head*, about a couple dealing with one person's meth addiction. Carina Round sings the verses, with Curt taking the chorus. The verses have a freneticism to them before it gives way to a reassuring lullaby of a chorus. Initially, it was going to be the other way around and Curt was going to play the addict, but in the sleeve notes, Curt says 'Carina did it so much better than I ever could. I'm the voice of reason (there's a first)'. Carina Round's contribution emphasises the fact that Curt's solo band of this era is effectively the Tears For Fears touring line-up up to *The Tipping Point*.

'My Point Being' (Curt Smith, Charlton Pettus)

This is an elegiac number written in the wake of the passing of Curt's mother. The song is a moment of realisation that petty arguments do not matter when something like that happens, 'My point being words are wasted on us' Curt sings to his brothers. The vocals are tender and set against a sparse and melancholy electronic backing – a reflective moment on the album.

'All Is Love (Curt Smith, Charlton Pettus)

It opens with a light piano backing and that gives way to an electronic element from the second verse onwards. There's some beautiful instrumentation on this track and another trademark tender vocal from Curt, with female vocals low in the mix. The middle eight has a rockier element before it returns to the softer arrangement. Initially written as a theme tune for an animated TV show that was not made, Curt loved the song and put it to use here. The original was lacking the orchestral arrangement. Curt Smith reached out via Twitter to the musician Zoe Keating and she provided the beautiful cello arrangement that is a feature of the song.

'Porn Star' (Curt Smith, Charlton Pettus)

It is an overtly political song and one that deals with the American political system. It has a degree of prescience about it, seeing that it was written in the pre-Trump era. Instead, it was written in the Obama era and the realisation that the system in the US is broken and that money wins out. Curt is now a naturalised citizen of the US and sings about being 'in love, with a porn star', which is his metaphor for the system he is kicking against. The song has a breezy arrangement that belies the deceptively heavy subject matter. The guitar hooks draw in the listener and return throughout the song, while Curt's vocals are great as ever but sound like they have been processed to sound like they have been delivered by phone. It's his co-singer, Holly Palmer, that delivers the clearer chorus. The middle eight breaks down dramatically before it returns to the earlier tone of the song.

'Well Enough' (Curt Smith, Charlton Pettus)
The sombre and sometimes downbeat nature of the album could be down to the introspective mood that Smith was in at the time, written around the time of his mother's death. This is the most personal song on the album, composed on a flight home from the UK after his mother's funeral. The title is about his mum doing the best she could to raise Curt. As Curt says in the sleeve notes: 'Also, to me, the phrase summed up her solitary life bringing up three boys – well, enough, alone. Amazing what a comma can do'. The song features a delicately strummed guitar that compliments Curt's emotional vocal. Other musical textures slowly build throughout, before evocative Celtic tones are introduced at 2:02. They soon give way to the textures that can be heard in the early part of the song. The reflective mood of the song and the Celtic influences reveal Smith in a contemplative mood.

'Heaven's Sake' (Curt Smith, Charlton Pettus)
This song was written as one of Curt's stand-alone Christmas singles but he felt that it fitted in well with the overall tone of this album. The idea behind it is 'Occupy Christmas'. The song is not about the religious aspect of the holiday period but the commercialization of the period with cash registers somewhere in the mix. The song has a skittering rhythmic pattern, making it almost feels like a drum and bass track. It was also released separately as a standalone 'single' from the album and it's a family affair with members of the Pettus family acting as backing vocalists.

'Wild' (Curt Smith, Charlton Pettus)
Redressing the imbalance of having written one song for a daughter, this one was for his younger daughter, Wilder. He wrote it for what he described as the 'sometimes trying but the mostly adorable contrarian in our family.' The song opens with a delicate arrangement before the band kicks in. There is a percussive, oriental feel to the verses, which is underpinned by a decent bassline hook.

'Mannequin' (Curt Smith, Charlton Pettus)
The song is another sensitive one – written for his mother-in-law, who also passed away the year before the album came about. She suffered from manic depression/bipolar disorder her whole life. The line 'I love the manic in your

kind of crazy' is the 'up' period that he celebrates in this song, which has a two-pronged approach in its arrangement, including tender and skurrying sections. Despite the sad, reflective lyrics, it's a funky song, almost celebratory in style.

'Some Secrets' (Curt Smith, Charlton Pettus)
Cryptically the sleeve notes say '...Never should be told :)'. This is an affectionate closing number with lightly picked guitar and organ pulsing away in the background. The chorus has a lovely melody as Smith sings 'one for sorrow, two for joy' over a chilled arrangement. It is a nice way to end the album.

Stand Alone Singles, B-sides, EPs and Other Contemporary Tracks
Curt Smith (feat. Zöe Keating)
'All Is Love' (Curt Smith, Charlton Pettus)
This is an equally gentle version of the song, with cellist Zoë Keating getting credit for her telling contributions.

'Perfectly ... Still' (featuring Universal Hall Pass) (Curt Smith, Charlton Pettus)
This was to be the second single for an album of collaborations with artists that Curt Smith met via social media. The single promised so much but the project was not fully realised. Perhaps his other commitments got in the way as the Tears For Fears touring schedule kicked up a gear in this period. Smith met guest artist Universal Hall Pass (Melissa R. Kaplan) after one of his fans responded to a request for collaborator suggestions by tweeting: 'Can I please be a complete slobbering fangirl and recommend the ethereal Melissa Kaplan?' Smith was equally impressed and got in touch with Kaplan via Myspace. After she wouldn't believe that he was who he claimed to be, he convinced her that he was the real deal and they agreed to participate. Smith sent Kaplan the in-progress tracks, to which she added both vocals and instrumentation without ever meeting her in person.

The song is a story of a man who has a good family and home life but is tempted to throw it all away for a potential exotic relationship in a different country. It's a cautionary tale that when the protagonist's mind settles down, he realises what he will lose. The song was released on 12 August 2010.

Holiday Songs
This is a download EP of three of the holiday songs, featuring 'Amazing Grace', 'Silent Night, and 'This Is Christmas' released November 29, 2010.

'Amazing Grace' (John Newton)
Curt Smith takes on this perennial song associated with funerals in a period when he had recorded a few songs that dealt with mortality. It is a beautifully

understated version. He offered it as his free download for the 2009 holiday period.

'Silent Night' (Franz Xaver Gruber, Joseph Mohr)
It was his first-holiday offering that he recorded back in 2008 and distributed free. It's a beautifully understated version of the song, suiting Curt's tenor. He is ably assisted on backing vocals by Gaby Moreno. It was produced by Smith and the 'Reverend' Charlton Pettus.

'This Is Christmas' (Curt Smith, Charlton Pettus)
Despite the perceived wisdom that all the great Christmas songs have been written, this is a decent stab at writing a contemporary one. It will have you trying to find out who did the original of the song, but no one did; it's a Smith/Pettus collaboration originally released in November 2010. According to Smith, the song tells the story 'of an adult visiting his parents at Christmas and lamenting how he's always made to feel like a child when he returns home. It culminates in his realization and acceptance that they're family after all, and nothing will (or even should) change that.'

It's a real family affair with backing vocalists including Smith's daughters Diva and Wilder. Collaborator Charlton Pettus' children Georgica and Harry join in, as well as a chorus comprising of local school children (Lisa P's 6th Grade Classes), plus Jason Joseph and Simon Steadman.

As well as having a solo career post Tears For Fears, Curt Smith has acted. One regular appearance was playing an exaggerated version of himself in the US TV show *Psych*. 'This Is Christmas' was featured in an episode of that show in December 2010. This inclusion prompted the song to come together. 'I'd been attempting to write a holiday song for years,' Smith says, 'but always found them a bit trite and forced. I was trying again when *Psych*'s James Roday approached me about licensing a song for the holiday episode of *Psych*. Once he sent me a clip of the scene he had in mind, it all made sense and the song came together naturally.' It's a beautiful song to sing along to, with minimalist backing.

Roland Orzabal Solo and Other Projects

Tomcats Screaming Outside

Personnel:
Roland Orzabal: Guitar, keyboards, programming, vocals
Alan Griffiths: Guitar, keyboards, programming
David Sutton: Bass
Nick D'Virgilio: Drums
Record label: Eagle/ Gold Circle
Recorded: Roland Orzabal & Alan Griffiths
UK Release Date: April 2001 (UK) September 2001 (US)
Highest Chart Placings: did not chart
Run Time: 54:35

There is only one solo record that bears the name of Roland Orzabal, although some people say that they class *Elemental* and *Raoul and the Kings of Spain* as solo records, of course. On the other hand, *Tomcats Screaming Outside* is a solo record, but it feels like it could easily have been a Tears For Fears record – the sort of album that the band might have been making at the turn of the century.

The album came out at a time when it made sense for Orzabal to try something different as an artist. Tears For Fears was not cutting through the noise beyond their loyal fanbase. There had been a sense of diminishing returns in terms of sales, even if this hadn't been reflected in the quality of their output as far as fans were concerned. When that happens to a band, it is a hard thing to turn around. It is interesting to think what would have happened if this album had followed *Elemental* as a Tears For Fears release and *Raoul and the Kings of Spain* was badged as a solo album instead.

The project came as a result of wanting to start again. Orzabal was fed up with the 'same old song going round and around'. It was on a Tears For Fears tour in 1996 in Bogata that things came to a head. The fans loved the gigs, but the logistics were poor. Orzabal said of that experience: 'At the end of the show, it was just phenomenal. Yet during the encores, in my mind, I said, 'I've had enough of this'. The whole history of Tears For Fears'.

Orzabal slipped away from it all into a period of semi-retirement as he spent time with his children; for a while, he was more interested in the father role than that of being a pop star. Even though he had put Tears For Fears on hold, he had made contact with Curt Smith after nine years. Relations had been slowly improving between the pair, but as yet, there was no sense that a new Tears For Fears album, with or without his original partner, was on the cards.

He also busied himself writing music, without any view to releasing anything. He started producing songs with little or no lyrical depth. He did not want to write anything too personal, somewhat different from his previous working style. Having worked as a producer with Icelandic / Italian

129

singer-songwriter Emilíana Torrini, that experience also acted as a catalyst for this album. He said to *Record Collector* before release:

> I knew I had to go away and try something else. Get away from the whole subject material, which has been pretty consistent from the beginning; try and go into different areas, and it took a while. I wanted to take away the burden and history of Tears For Fears. I'm not saying that in the future there won't be another Tears For Fears album; there quite possibly will be. I wanted for this one to take the pressure off, remove the Sword of Damocles that's been over my head after every album, and just see where it goes and how it would feel to cut off from the past a little. Not worry about the commercial aspects; how many records are going to sell, and that rubbish. Just try on another suit of clothes for a while.

He told the journalist Katherine Kelly that title came from overhearing something that his then-wife, Caroline had said: 'As she went out the door, she said, 'Tomcat screaming outside'. She said 'Tomcat', but I heard it as 'Tomcats screaming outside' and I thought, 'hmmm...that's it!'"

Two of the mainstays of Tears For Fears' second period were present and the Roland Orzabal and Alan Griffiths partnership was renewed for their third album together. Nick D'Virgilio, from prog-rockers Spock's Beard, was brought in as the drummer, having previously drummed for Tears For Fears on the *Raoul and the Kings of Spain* tours. He would later do so on the *Everybody Loves a Happy Ending* tour.

The lack of the Tears For Fears baggage resulted in an album that has a different sonic vibe, although there are a few of the trademark melodic gems littered across it. Again, bad luck got in the way of this being more successful. It was released in America on the day of the 9/11 attacks, lessening any chance that it had of making an impact over there. The album was warmly received by the band's loyal followers, but once again, it would not bring in a new audience. The label at the time did not push the album, which is why it is not known beyond the fanbase.

The front cover has Orzabal in sunglasses in what looks like a fairly urban and industrial setting. The picture has a brown tint and another figure can be seen in the background.

'Ticket to the World' (Roland Orzabal, Alan Griffiths)

One of the ideas behind this solo album is that it should be different rhythmically, and the opening number certainly demonstrates that perfectly. The bassline and the drumming were markedly different to what had gone before. Orzabal had always utilised technology in his songwriting, but this was always in the standard rock/pop format. This time he used programmed beats that were influenced by the then contemporary sound of drum&bass, although the guitar and vocals could easily sit on a Tears For Fears release. The guitar line at the start has a hook that draws the listener in, while the chiming, jangly guitars give way to the pounding bassline that drives the song along. Lyrically, it is hard to pin down what the song is about, there are a few interesting lines. If the plan was to park the meaning and focus on something more about rhythm, then this song works quite well and might have been a safer choice as a first single, given that it acts as a perfect bridge in sound between Tears For Fears and Orzabal as a solo artist.

'Low Life' (Roland Orzabal)

This was the debut solo single for Orzabal and the first to be taken from the album. It was released as a single in the US and Germany and as a promotional single in the UK. The full UK release was scrapped at the last minute. The different approach to songwriting is noticeable on this track, with a different rhythmic feel, but Orzabal's distinctive vocals remain. The track opens with a pulsing rhythm and a sample of a middle eastern choir. This rhythm is consistent throughout the song, with treated guitars throughout. There are four tracks on the single, which includes the: 'album version', 'supersub mix', 'and president who? Mix', and 'radio edit'., although these differ only slightly from the main release. A video directed by Jo Tanner accompanies the song, though it bears little relation to the track itself.

'Hypnoculture' (Roland Orzabal)

Now, this one would surprise people who had stumbled on the album expecting something in the same mode as a Tears For Fears release. For a start, the vocals don't kick in until two minutes into the song. The standard verse-chorus-verse-chorus structure is parked for something more rhythmic and ambient. There is a sample track that opens the song that has an Arabic, middle eastern vibe. The bassline is the force that drives the song before it gives way to a light vocal from Orzabal.

'Bullets for Brains' (Roland Orzabal, Alan Griffiths)

Again, this is something that could have been released under the name of Tears For Fears. It would have fitted nicely on the *Elemental* album. There is an epic quality to the song that is synonymous with some of their classic hits. There's a catchy riff that gives the song its hook, although there is an electronic pulse that makes the song feel at home with the sonic template of the rest of the album. Even though lyrically, it feels like this is nothing more than a series of arresting couplets, it could be a song that looks at the contradictions of religious dogma.

'For the Love of Cain' (Roland Orzabal)

This was earmarked as the second single from the album, but it was shelved and released on a limited basis through Orzabal's website. It has a slow-building verse that hits one of the sing-along choruses that Orzabal has made

131

a speciality throughout his career. This does sound like the most conventional song on the album. The chorus is very much in keeping with Orzabal's previous style. The intro has an Americana-style melodica riff and guitars that lead into the verse. There are yet more religious references throughout the lyrics of the song, as well as the title itself. The drums seem to be quite prominent in the mix. Drum & bass? This is more drum and vocal.

'Under Ether' (Roland Orzabal, Alan Griffiths)

This is one of the more experiential numbers. There is a haunting middle-eastern-influences guitar riff that opens the song. The drums and bass intertwine with a guitar pattern that runs throughout the song, which is less about the big chorus, and more about atmosphere and the ambience. It is sprawling and the longest cut on the album. Lyrically, it's another difficult song to pin down. Is it about science? Is it about political protest? is it about climate change? It is an arresting number that sits nicely in the overall flow of the record.

'Day By Day by Day By Day By Day' (Roland Orzabal, Alan Griffiths)

This is quite a mellow, ambient, at some points trip-hop inflected number. If a second solo album had been released, it would have been good to hear similar songs of this nature. There is a laid-back vocal over a fairly minimalist musical figure from Orzabal. The atmosphere has a dreamy, relaxing, chillout feel to it.

'Dandelion' (Roland Orzabal, Alan Griffiths)

This opens with a heavy distorted repetitive guitar. It has a sparse riff that opens each verse. It is probably one of the weaker and more straightforward songs on the album – and it's the shortest number too – an out-and-out rocker. It's all quite conventional, despite the occasional electronic flourish. Lyrically it employs word association over meaning, although 'does time stand still if you're stuck in a wormhole?' again references Orzabal's love for physics and popular science.

'Hey Andy!' (Roland Orzabal)

This is very much in keeping with the drum&bass and experiential style that was envisaged by Orzabal in the making of this album. It's a good experimental number with a deeper hidden meaning in the song. 'God played dice and called you home', references a friend's death at a time when several other deaths of people close to Orzabal occurred in the lead-up to the album's release – notably his wife Caroline's parents. The line 'Hey Andy/When I die, you'll be waiting for me' sees Orzabal trying to get an understanding of these events. The song works well within the style of the album overall, and a skittering beat hangs about throughout. It is the purest of the drum&bass songs on the album.

'Kill Love' (Roland Orzabal, Alan Griffiths)

This is another sonic departure, while lyrically, the song questions what Orzabal was doing as a musician. Perhaps questioning the way that the album itself was going. 'The same old song going around and around and it's not where I'm at, it's just where I found myself, still, the sounds keep the wolves from the door.' Interviewed at the time by *Record Collector* he said 'I'm doing a drum and bass track here, and it still sounds like me! What do I have to do to stop sounding like me?'. It is quite an atmospheric track and one that, despite Orzabal's uncertainty, works well. It has a busy electronic pulse running through the song and a delicate piano riff that acts as the hook.

'Snowdrop' (Roland Orzabal, Alan Griffiths)

The song is quite minimalist, hung together with a drum pattern and a sparse riff, almost acting as a continuation of the previous song; a comedown. There's a strong vocal from Orzabal that acts as the hook of the song; it is much needed, given the sparse arrangement.

'Maybe Our Days Are Numbered' (Roland Orzabal, Alan Griffiths)

The standout track on the album and it should have been released as a single. There is a beautifully delicate vocal from Orzabal with an equally slight keyboard riff in the background. It's a strong song that fits in with the sonic textures of the rest of the album and yet the listener yearns to hear it played by Tears For Fears. It does not deserve to be lost in the relative obscurity of this album. It appears to be about a love gone wrong; it might be about being unsure as to whether to end a relationship. It was covered by Rare Futures in 2021, who did a fairly faithful rendition of the song and is well worth checking out.

Stand Alone Singles, B-sides, EPs and Other Contemporary Tracks

Two singles were associated with the album in 'Low Life' and 'For the Love of Cain'. These releases included other tracks that could be found on the album and various alternative mixes.

Other Credits (Production and Writing)

As well as being an accomplished songwriter Roland Orzabal has also served as a producer on several albums and songs down the years away from Tears For Fears releases.

One of his earliest production credits can be found on a Blue Hat Records release in 1979 of 'Boogie Town (Planet Venus)' by the Poole Family. This was engineered by Glen Tommey, who would later produce (along with Tony Hatch) Graduate's debut album.

Having met and invited Oleta Adams to perform with Tears For Fears, it made sense for her to release an album of her own on the back of her successful collaboration. The fruits of that union were the 1990 album *Circle of One*, which Roland co-produced with David Bascombe. It spawned the worldwide hit 'Get Here,' which was a cover of the Brenda Russell song. It gained some poignancy during the Gulf War when it was released in 1991, when it was adopted as an anthem by the US troops. Besides the production, there was only one songwriting contribution on the album from Orzabal, which was the album's opening track, 'Rhythm of Life', also given a dance-friendly remix by DJ William Orbit.

'Rhythm of Life' is a co-write with Nicky Holland and stems from the protracted *The Seeds of Love* sessions. It had been in the running on the album but was superseded by other songs. A version of the original demo can be heard on the Super Deluxe Edition Box Set of *The Seeds of Love*.

Orzabal teamed up with the Icelandic singer Emilíana Torrini to co-produce (with Alan Griffiths) her third album *Love in a Time of Science*. The album was released in 1999 and 2000 in the US, with the majority recorded at Neptune's Kitchen, Orzabal's home studio – there was some additional recording in Spain and Iceland. It is an electronica and trip-hop flavoured album with Roland providing backing vocals and some instrumentation. He makes two songwriting contributions in the form of 'Wednesday's Child', which is a keyboard-led trip-hop number with a dreamy, laid-back quality to it and 'Baby Blue', which has the guitars quite prominently at the start before the descending chords return to another similarly laid-back number, before the chorus ramps things up again. The overall sound and the processes inspired the tone of Orzabal's *Tomcats Screaming Outside*.

Tear For Fears Live Projects

In My Mind's Eye. Live a Hammersmith Odeon (1983) (Video/ DVD/Laserdisc)

The band's first long-form video was recorded in December 1983 and released in 1984 on home video.

The collection contains songs from the first album, as well as tracks such as 'Mother's Talk', 'The Working Hour' and 'Head Over Heels', while 'We Are Broken', the song that would go on to become 'Broken' and bookends 'Head Over Heels', on the *Songs from the Big Chair* album is played in its earliest incarnation. The live element of that song is taken from this release.

As a concert performance, it is a good snapshot of the band developing their live sound, shaped by a group of musicians who would go on to help record the next album. What has not held up in the intervening years is the 80s graphics. The concert video itself was directed by Mike Mansfield. Curt Smith and Roland Orzabal were less than happy with the video release in general, particularly the visual effects added to it.

The band recorded a fuller set that night, but it has been edited for release. Notably missing from the set is the band's then-single 'The Way You Are'.

The performance has had a TV audience – it was shown on television in the UK in March 1985 as part of Channel 4's *Mirror Image* programme. The broadcast featured an even more reduced track list but included an interview with the band, while the VHS was originally only released on videocassette and laserdisc, although it was released on DVD as part of the 30th anniversary 4-disc super deluxe edition box set of *The Hurting* in October 2013.

Tracklist: 'Start of the Breakdown', 'Mothers Talk', 'Pale Shelter', 'The Working Hour', 'The Prisoner', 'Ideas As Opiates', 'Mad World', 'We Are Broken', 'Head Over Heels', 'Suffer The Children', 'The Hurting', 'Memories Fade', 'Change'

Going to California (1990) (Video/DVD)

This is the band's second long-form concert release, capturing the band's gig at the Santa Barbara County Bowl, US, in May 1990 during *The Seeds of Love* world tour.

The gig featured Curt Smith and Roland Orzabal alongside the touring band of the time, which included Oleta Adams (piano and vocals), Carol Steele (percussion and backing vocals), Neil Taylor (lead guitar), Andy Davis (keyboards), Will Gregory (saxophone), Jim Copley (drums), Adele Bertei (backing vocals), and Biti Strauchn (backing vocals).

It captured the band on its last tour in the original partnership. It has a grainy quality to it, almost like it was trying to mimic a bootleg experience. The concert footage was directed by Nigel Dick, who had previously worked with the band on several videos throughout the *Songs from the Big Chair* era.

The sound of the band is more expansive than it had been for previous releases, highlighting the musical maturity shown with the release of *The Seeds of Love*. It is noticeable that it's not Roland or Curt that open the proceedings, but Oleta Adams, who performs a version of 'I Believe' with a few of the backing band.

'Change' undergoes a big development with this outing and it contains a rap from Biti Strauchn, while Oleta Adams chips in with elements of the 'Mothers Talk' lyrics. 'Famous Last Words' has 'When the Saints Go Marching In' appended on the end. In keeping with the band's love of The Beatles, they do a decent version of 'All You Need Is Love'. They adapt some of the lyrics to incorporate some of the themes that can be found on *The Seeds of Love* and we get the first mention of 'Raoul and the Kings of Spain'.

Since it was first released on video and laserdisc, it has also been released in 2005 as a double pack DVD with the *Scenes from the Big Chair* documentary.

Tracklist: 'Women of Ireland' (instrumental), 'I Believe' (performed by Oleta Adams), 'Head Over Heels' / 'Broken', 'Change', 'Pale Shelter', 'Woman in Chains', 'Advice for the Young at Heart', 'Mad World', 'Famous Last Words' / 'When the Saints Go Marching In', 'I've Got to Sing My Song' (performed by Oleta Adams), 'Badman's Song', 'Sowing the Seeds of Love' 'All You Need Is Love', 'Everybody Wants to Rule the World', 'Year of the Knife', 'Shout'.

Live from Santa Barbara (2009) (CD/DVD)
Release date: 15th December 2009
Label: Immortal
A cheap quality release of highlights from the original *Going to California – Live from Santa Barbara* concert. There are some curious omissions from the original version.

Tracklisting: 'I Believe' (performed by Oleta Adams), 'Head Over Heels' (as well as 'Broken' which is not listed), 'Woman in Chains', 'Year of the Knife', 'Advice for the Young at Heart', 'Sowing the Seeds of Love', 'Badman's Song', 'Famous Last Words', 'When the Saints Go Marching In', 'I've Got to Sing My Song' (performed by Oleta Adams), 'Shout', 'Everybody Wants to Rule the World'

Secret World Live in Paris (2006) (CD/DVD)
Personnel:
Roland Orzabal: guitar and vocals
Curt Smith: vocal and bass guitar
Charlton Pettus: lead guitar
Doug Petty: keyboards
Nick D'Virgilio: drums
Record label: XIII Bis Recordings

Release Date: 27 February 2006
Run Time: 57:05

This is rare – the first live album that the band had released. It has contained nine live versions of classics from the band's back catalogue, plus three bonus studio tracks. The live album was recorded at the Parc des Princes stadium in Paris, France, during their 2005 world tour and was released on 27 February 2006 by the French record label XIII Bis. The two-disc release contains the CD album along with a DVD video of the performance, which replicates the track listing of the live cuts on the CD.

There are three additional studio tracks; the previously unreleased 'Floating Down the River,' a radio edit of 'Secret World' (released as a promo single in France) and 'What Are We Fighting For?', a song written and originally included on Curt Smith's 1998 album *Mayfield*.

There are a few subtle variations to some of the live versions. 'Secret World', which is the live opening track on the release, contains elements of Paul McCartney's 'Let 'Em In' in the elongated instrumental part of the song. 'Closest Thing to Heaven' starts with Charlton Pettus playing an ebow to get a nice drone effect, which is put to good use on a different take on their first hit 'Mad World', attempting to capture the slow-building style of Michael Andrews and Gary Jules cover version of the song.

'Floating Down the River' (Roland Orzabal)

This is another curio from the band's back catalogue. It is a knockabout number and sounds like it was written during the *Everybody Loves Happy Ending* sessions and was earmarked to be an extra on a new greatest hits package or an expanded anthology on the Universal label. This comprehensive release never came out, although the song did appear in the label's subsidiary Gold's budget compilation. It has elements of the Beatlesque sound that the band were aiming at in this period, while the synth patterns of the chorus sound similar to the Paul Weller song 'It's Written in the Stars'. It's a great song – indeed, the whole release is worth getting hold of as a representation of a live gig from the latter period of the band.

Tracklist; Live Tracks: 'Secret World', 'Call Me Mellow', 'Sowing the Seeds of Love', 'Pale Shelter', 'Closest Thing to Heaven', 'Mad World', 'Everybody Wants to Rule the World', 'Head over Heels', 'Shout'. Bonus Tracks: 'Secret World' (radio edit), 'Floating Down the River' (previously unreleased), 'What Are We Fighting For' (previously released on Curt Smith's 1998 *Mayfield* album)

Live at Massey Hall Toronto, Canada/1985 (Vinyl LP/CD) (2021)

2021 Record Store Day release (CD/vinyl)
Release date: 12 June 2021
Label: UMC / Mercury Records Limited

Tears For Fears' contribution to Record Store Day 2021 was the release of *Live at Massey Hall Toronto, Canada/ 1985*. It was an extremely limited release on both CD and Vinyl and it captures 13 of the songs that the band performed that night. For some reason, it omits 'Change' and the 'Start of the Breakdown', which were the band's encores.

Elements of the concert have been released before. Footage from the gig can be seen in *Scenes from the Big Chair*, released in 1985 and some of the audio tracks have appeared on the *Songs from the Big Chair* super deluxe edition box set.

The album captures the band at the height of their success in the mid-80s. The band sound tight and focused and those in attendance were treated to a vintage performance. The dialogue on the album hints at the fact that a number of the fans queued up overnight to get tickets and see the gig. They would no doubt be impressed with what they witnessed.

Tracklisting: 'Mothers Talk', 'Broken', 'Head Over Heels' / 'Broken', 'Pale Shelter', 'Memories Fade', 'Start of the Breakdown', 'The Prisoner', 'I Believe', 'The Working Hour', 'Mad World', 'Everybody Wants to Rule the World', 'The Hurting', 'Shout'

The Big Black Smoke

Label: Iconography
Release date: May 6 2022
Run Time: 81 minutes

The Big Black Smoke is a live album that captures the band at two stages of their early career, with the 2022 release timed to capitalise on the success of *The Tipping Point*.

The 16-track album has two gigs, one from June 10 1985, recorded at Hammersmith Odeon in London and a second gig from April 18 1983, recorded at Hammersmith Palais. The compilation captures several songs from the first two albums and was recorded for radio shows, one of which was the *King Biscuit Flower Hour* radio show, an American syndicated radio show that specialised in broadcasting live concerts (it's unclear if both shows appeared on the same programme).

The first eight tracks are predominately from the *Songs from the Big Chair* era and have all the hits that you would expect from that time. It's not a full set of songs from the night but a selection that people with only a passing knowledge of the band would know. Two songs from *The Hurting* era are listed – the title track and 'Suffer the Children'.

The remaining tracks are from 1983 and focus mainly on tracks from the debut album. 'The Hurting' is included for a second time, and curiously 'The Way You Are' is included, which is a selling point as the song very rarely sees the light of day in any form.

The album appears on the Iconography label, which seems to specialise in releasing live radio gigs and other semi-official releases. The sleeve notes are limited with a biography that seems to stop at *Everybody Loves a Happy Ending*. There is a front cover from UK pop magazine *Smash Hits* featuring the band that makes up the other page on the inside of the sleeve notes. The sound quality is reasonably good and the band sound great live on both nights, although there is no pretence that this is the full set as the songs are edited so that they fade the crowd noise at the end of each song.

Given that there have been other live albums by the band that have been issued in other territories, unofficially or on a limited basis, the album is a good stop-gap to satisfy the demand for an officially sanctioned live release. Maybe that will come at the end of *The Tipping Point* tour, but for now, this compilation is a good way of listening to the band in its earliest incarnations.

Tracklisting: (Tracks 1-8) A Live FM Broadcast Record at Hammersmith Odeon 10 June 1985: 'Mothers Talk', 'Broken'/'Head Over Heels', 'Memories Fade', 'Mad World', 'Everybody Wants to Rule the World', 'The Hurting', 'Shout', 'Suffer The Children' (Tracks 9-16), A Live FM Broadcast Record at Hammersmith Palais 18th April 1983: Memories Fade', 'The Way You Are', 'Pale Shelter', 'The Prisoner', 'Ideas As Opiates', 'Change', 'Start of the Breakdown', 'The Hurting'.

Documentaries

Scenes from the Big Chair

Label: Phonogram Records
Release date: November 1985
Run Time: 75 minutes

Scenes from the Big Chair is the classic 'band on tour' documentary that bands used to put out for the then-burgeoning home video market to cash in on their success. The film captured the band at the height of their powers during the *Songs from the Big Chair* era. The documentary is a mix of the videos from the time and backstage/tour bus footage featuring interviews with members of the touring band and not just Roland and Curt. There is also on-the-road footage as they travel through Europe and North America as well as TV spots for Japanese television programmes.

It was put together by Nigel Dick, the band's long-term director and it shows the harmonious side of the band's whirlwind world tour. In the moments that the band are captured in the live setting, they sound great and on top of their game.

The film also contains a selection of videos from that era, including 'Shout' and 'Everybody Wants to Rule the World'. Plus, the making of the 'Head over Heels' video, which was filmed during the time the band was touring in Canada at the time they did the Massey Hall gig in Toronto in May 1985.

Scenes from the Big Chair was originally released in 1985 on video and laserdisc. It was later released on DVD in 2005 and the extras include the full *Going to California* concert performance which was recorded during the band's *The Seeds of Love* World Tour in May 1990, which was also directed by Nigel Dick and available for the first time on DVD. It also contained an interview with Chris Hughes recorded in 2005. It was subsequently reissued on DVD in 2014 as part of the six-disc Super Deluxe Edition of *Songs from the Big Chair*.

On Track series
Alan Parsons Project – Steve Swift 978-1-78952-154-2
Tori Amos – Lisa Torem 978-1-78952-142-9
Asia – Peter Braidis 978-1-78952-099-6
Badfinger – Robert Day-Webb 978-1-878952-176-4
Barclay James Harvest – Keith and Monica Domone 978-1-78952-067-5
The Beatles – Andrew Wild 978-1-78952-009-5
The Beatles Solo 1969-1980 – Andrew Wild 978-1-78952-030-9
Blue Oyster Cult – Jacob Holm-Lupo 978-1-78952-007-1
Blur – Matt Bishop – 978-178952-164-1
Marc Bolan and T.Rex – Peter Gallagher 978-1-78952-124-5
Kate Bush – Bill Thomas 978-1-78952-097-2
Camel – Hamish Kuzminski 978-1-78952-040-8
Caravan – Andy Boot 978-1-78952-127-6
Cardiacs – Eric Benac 978-1-78952-131-3
Eric Clapton Solo – Andrew Wild 978-1-78952-141-2
The Clash – Nick Assirati 978-1-78952-077-4
Crosby, Stills and Nash – Andrew Wild 978-1-78952-039-2
The Damned – Morgan Brown 978-1-78952-136-8
Deep Purple and Rainbow 1968-79 – Steve Pilkington 978-1-78952-002-6
Dire Straits – Andrew Wild 978-1-78952-044-6
The Doors – Tony Thompson 978-1-78952-137-5
Dream Theater – Jordan Blum 978-1-78952-050-7
Electric Light Orchestra – Barry Delve 978-1-78952-152-8
Elvis Costello and The Attractions – Georg Purvis 978-1-78952-129-0
Emerson Lake and Palmer – Mike Goode 978-1-78952-000-2
Fairport Convention – Kevan Furbank 978-1-78952-051-4
Peter Gabriel – Graeme Scarfe 978-1-78952-138-2
Genesis – Stuart MacFarlane 978-1-78952-005-7
Gentle Giant – Gary Steel 978-1-78952-058-3
Gong – Kevan Furbank 978-1-78952-082-8
Hall and Oates – Ian Abrahams 978-1-78952-167-2
Hawkwind – Duncan Harris 978-1-78952-052-1
Peter Hammill – Richard Rees Jones 978-1-78952-163-4
Roy Harper – Opher Goodwin 978-1-78952-130-6
Jimi Hendrix – Emma Stott 978-1-78952-175-7
The Hollies – Andrew Darlington 978 1 78952-159-7
Iron Maiden – Steve Pilkington 978-1-78952-061-3
Jefferson Airplane – Richard Butterworth 978-1-78952-143-6
Jethro Tull – Jordan Blum 978-1-78952-016-3
Elton John in the 1970s – Peter Kearns 978-1-78952-034-7
The Incredible String Band – Tim Moon 978-1-78952-107-8
Iron Maiden – Steve Pilkington 978-1-78952-061-3
Judas Priest – John Tucker 978-1-78952-018-7

Also available from Sonicbond

Kansas – Kevin Cummings 978-1-78952-057-6
The Kinks – Martin Hutchinson 978-1-78952-172-6
Korn – Matt Karpe 978-1-78952-153-5
Led Zeppelin – Steve Pilkington 978-1-78952-151-1
Level 42 – Matt Philips 978-1-78952-102-3
Little Feat – 978-1-78952-168-9
Aimee Mann – Jez Rowden 978-1-78952-036-1
Joni Mitchell – Peter Kearns 978-1-78952-081-1
The Moody Blues – Geoffrey Feakes 978-1-78952-042-2
Motorhead – Duncan Harris 978-1-78952-173-3
Mike Oldfield – Ryan Yard 978-1-78952-060-6
Opeth – Jordan Blum 978-1-78-952-166-5
Tom Petty – Richard James 978-1-78952-128-3
Porcupine Tree – Nick Holmes 978-1-78952-144-3
Queen – Andrew Wild 978-1-78952-003-3
Radiohead – William Allen 978-1-78952-149-8
Renaissance – David Detmer 978-1-78952-062-0
The Rolling Stones 1963-80 – Steve Pilkington 978-1-78952-017-0
The Smiths and Morrissey – Tommy Gunnarsson 978-1-78952-140-5
Status Quo the Frantic Four Years – Richard James 978-1-78952-160-3
Steely Dan – Jez Rowden 978-1-78952-043-9
Steve Hackett – Geoffrey Feakes 978-1-78952-098-9
Thin Lizzy – Graeme Stroud 978-1-78952-064-4
Toto – Jacob Holm-Lupo 978-1-78952-019-4
U2 – Eoghan Lyng 978-1-78952-078-1
UFO – Richard James 978-1-78952-073-6
The Who – Geoffrey Feakes 978-1-78952-076-7
Roy Wood and the Move – James R Turner 978-1-78952-008-8
Van Der Graaf Generator – Dan Coffey 978-1-78952-031-6
Yes – Stephen Lambe 978-1-78952-001-9
Frank Zappa 1966 to 1979 – Eric Benac 978-1-78952-033-0
Warren Zevon – Peter Gallagher 978-1-78952-170-2
10CC – Peter Kearns 978-1-78952-054-5

Decades Series
The Bee Gees in the 1960s – Andrew Mon Hughes et al 978-1-78952-148-1
The Bee Gees in the 1970s – Andrew Mon Hughes et al 978-1-78952-179-5
Black Sabbath in the 1970s – Chris Sutton 978-1-78952-171-9
Britpop – Peter Richard Adams and Matt Pooler 978-1-78952-169-6
Alice Cooper in the 1970s – Chris Sutton 978-1-78952-104-7
Curved Air in the 1970s – Laura Shenton 978-1-78952-069-9
Bob Dylan in the 1980s – Don Klees 978-1-78952-157-3
Fleetwood Mac in the 1970s – Andrew Wild 978-1-78952-105-4
Focus in the 1970s – Stephen Lambe 978-1-78952-079-8
Free and Bad Company in the 1970s – John Van der Kiste 978-1-78952-178-8

Genesis in the 1970s – Bill Thomas 978178952-146-7
George Harrison in the 1970s – Eoghan Lyng 978-1-78952-174-0
Marillion in the 1980s – Nathaniel Webb 978-1-78952-065-1
Mott the Hoople and Ian Hunter in the 1970s – John Van der Kiste
978-1-78-952-162-7
Pink Floyd In The 1970s – Georg Purvis 978-1-78952-072-9
Tangerine Dream in the 1970s – Stephen Palmer 978-1-78952-161-0
The Sweet in the 1970s – Darren Johnson from Gary Cosby collection 978-1-
78952-139-9
Uriah Heep in the 1970s – Steve Pilkington 978-1-78952-103-0
Yes in the 1980s – Stephen Lambe with David Watkinson 978-1-78952-125-2

On Screen series
Carry On... – Stephen Lambe 978-1-78952-004-0
David Cronenberg – Patrick Chapman 978-1-78952-071-2
Doctor Who: The David Tennant Years – Jamie Hailstone 978-1-78952-066-8
James Bond – Andrew Wild – 978-1-78952-010-1
Monty Python – Steve Pilkington 978-1-78952-047-7
Seinfeld Seasons 1 to 5 – Stephen Lambe 978-1-78952-012-5

Other Books
1967: A Year In Psychedelic Rock – Kevan Furbank 978-1-78952-155-9
1970: A Year In Rock – John Van der Kiste 978-1-78952-147-4
1973: The Golden Year of Progressive Rock 978-1-78952-165-8
Babysitting A Band On The Rocks – G.D. Praetorius 978-1-78952-106-1
Eric Clapton Sessions – Andrew Wild 978-1-78952-177-1
Derek Taylor: For Your Radioactive Children – Andrew Darlington
978-1-78952-038-5
The Golden Road: The Recording History of The Grateful Dead – John Kilbride
978-1-78952-156-6
Iggy and The Stooges On Stage 1967-1974 – Per Nilsen 978-1-78952-101-6
Jon Anderson and the Warriors – the road to Yes – David Watkinson
978-1-78952-059-0
Nu Metal: A Definitive Guide – Matt Karpe 978-1-78952-063-7
Tommy Bolin: In and Out of Deep Purple – Laura Shenton 978-1-78952-070-5
Maximum Darkness – Deke Leonard 978-1-78952-048-4
Maybe I Should've Stayed In Bed – Deke Leonard 978-1-78952-053-8
The Twang Dynasty – Deke Leonard 978-1-78952-049-1

and many more to come!

Would you like to write for Sonicbond Publishing?
We are mainly a music publisher, but we also occasionally
publish in other genres including film and television. At Sonicbond
Publishing we are always on the look-out for authors, particularly for
our two main series, On Track and Decades.

Mixing fact with in depth analysis, the On Track series examines
the entire recorded work of a particular musical artist or group. All
genres are considered from easy listening and jazz to 60s soul to 90s
pop, via rock and metal.

The Decades series singles out a particular decade in an artist or
group's history and focuses on that decade in more detail than may
be allowed in the On Track series.

While professional writing experience would, of course, be
an advantage, the most important qualification is to have real
enthusiasm and knowledge of your subject. First-time authors are
welcomed, but the ability to write well in English is essential.

Sonicbond Publishing has distribution throughout Europe and
North America, and all our books are also published in E-book form.
Authors will be paid a royalty based on sales of their book.
Further details about our books are available from
www.sonicbondpublishing.com. To contact us, complete the
contact form there or email info@sonicbondpublishing.co.uk

are correct but less sincere, glorying in publicity. Others are sincere, but ultimately incorrect, perhaps coming forward because of mental instability or greed.' David Munyakei was both correct and sincere, since something was clearly rotten at the Central Bank and he wanted to change the organization. But perhaps David Munyakei was too sincere. For when the first Goldenberg story broke in the Nation, David Munyakei picked up the newspaper and leaped up at his desk. 'Yes, yes,' he shouted, waving the newspaper and the story. In that single moment he probably felt freed from months of self-doubt and fear. But he paid a price for that sincerity and, as his testimony shows, was not free for long.

Before he passed on, David Munyakei's mannerisms and speech had become sudden and discordant. He would talk without pacing himself, blurting out words with eyes open wide like someone who has been in the dark for a long time. Depending on the conversation he was given to sudden smiles that lit up his whole face. He was also given to sudden blank looks, often becoming lost in mid-sentence. He was always pre-occupied.

When these moods passed one felt his sense of entitlement. It was like something he was born with – like any blueblood who takes for granted his ascendancy in society: 'If you follow my history I would be very senior. I would have even been deputy governor. I belong to the managerial class,' he would say. He had come to realize his drawing power: 'I can call Onyango Jarmasai, I can call Paul Muite and Anyang' Nyong'o. I'm trying to make you see who I am – I can call Gibson Kamau Kuria. I can walk out of State House and enter a kiosk and eat githeri. This is what has helped me survive.'

He had delusions of grandeur, which in Kenya are

perhaps not far-fetched: 'I want to vie for MP in 2007,' he would say now and again. There are still several loose ends to David Munyakei's narrative. Incidents of shame in this theatre of the absurd.

Firstly, there was then, Justice Minister Kiraitu Murungi's order to David Sadera Munyakei to go back to work at the Central Bank of Kenya. This was during the Integrity Awards ceremony at the Safari Park Hotel in November 2004, in front of a large audience including then permanent secretary John Githongo. Afterwards, during the evening's cocktails several people came forward and promised David Munyakei all kinds of assistance.

None of them ever met or accepted an appointment to see David Munyakei. It is almost as if David had an intimation that nothing would result from Safari Park. It was a scene right out of the allegorical Animal Farm, where some of the farm animals have been momentarily elevated to social contact with the humans, sipping wine and clicking glasses. As David looked at the glass award he held in his hand he asked Felgona: 'Nitafanya nini na hii? Please keep it.' Felgona refused. What will I do with this award? Before his death David Munyakei ran into his former bosses Sisenda and Njoroge and he would say: 'Nikulalamika tuu. Nakusema niliwasitaki.' They just wring their hands complaining. Saying that I reported on them. On meeting Sisenda outside the 20th Century building, David was castigated for reporting what had been happening: 'Ulitustaki,' said Sisenda. In a later encounter, Njoroge maintained that he was innocent. To both David said, 'You must carry your own cross.'

Flashback to February 7th 2005. Another incident in the theatre of the absurd. David Munyakei received a phone call at Mama Jane's booth. The Kenyan Human

Rights Commission needed him in Nairobi. They were having their National Human Right Awards ceremony on the 18th of the same month. Could David grace them with his presence that evening? He wore The Suit. His life for those last weeks had been unraveling rather more than usual. After a serious domestic spat, his wife had left with the kids and was in Narok with his grandmother. On his way to the awards, he had attended talks to keep him and his wife and their kids under the same roof. Elders had been called.

All this was hardly evident as Munyakei received his award before First Lady Lucy Kibaki and Vice President Moody Awori. He did not mince his words and asked for his job back. Unlike Safari Park at the Integrity Awards not many came afterwards to offer congratulations - there had been at least 10 winners in different categories that evening. His 15 minutes of fame were almost up. A solitary old white lady came to Munyakei and wished him well. Looking around, Munyakei asked me to hold his hefty award statuette and rushed towards the centre of the room.

The leading lights that evening were the First Lady and the Vice President and everyone wanted to shake their hands. Munyakei came back with a grin. 'Hata hii haina cash,' he said, grabbing the heavy award. Even this one has no money. 'Lakini nimesalimia Lucy,' he added. But I've talked to Lucy. We headed towards the Norfolk Hibiscus bar. In the way through corridor outside, Munyakei exchanged pleasantries with Maina Kiai and Anyang' Nyong'o. Then he suddenly remembered: 'I have to talk to the accountant to get money for my hotel bill.'

I told him to he would find me at the bar and agreed to hold onto the award for him. Ten minutes later,

Munyakei was back. 'Accountant amesema cheque is not ready,' he said. Both of us were silent for a while, taking some downtime. While we were standing there, Munyakei started talking to a tall, bald, bulletheaded and bespectacled sharply dressed individual. Light blue shirt. Gold cuffs. Tie neatly held with a gold pin. Narrow titanium spectacles.

A Minister's son, I learnt later.

'Something must be done about this thing of yours,' I overheard him saying to Munyakei.

'Would you please repeat that,' I said butting into the conversation.

'And you are?' he peered over his glasses at me.

'I am a writer. Billy Kahora. I am writing about Munyakei's life.' His smile evaporated.

'I am not going to repeat anything. You people. I am not talking to you,' he said stabbing the air with a finger.

'You hear that …You hear that … Repeat what. I'm not repeating anything. Then you go lie and quote me.'

I was silent watching this outburst - brave new world, I thought. I noticed from the corner of my eye four white ladies, tourists, had noticed Munyakei's award. All aflutter they started oohing and aahing. And soon they had surrounded him, taking photos and fingering the award. I was left with the Minister's son. 'All of you people are crooked,' I was told. My amusement gradually turned into irritation: 'I did not come here to be lectured. You walk up to me... You hardly know who I am and you stand there and lecture me.' Taken aback he took a different tack. 'Let me ask you. What do you want for …?' he pointed at Munyakei. All efficient. Deal maker extraordinare. 'What do you want …? Say it. You claim that you want to help him. Tell me what you want.' Brave new world. I looked around at the soft seductive lights and plush light coloured velvet of the carpet and the deep sofas and thought how old the Norfolk was and probably how many such conversations like these had been held here since Kenya came into existence. Conversations between the entitled and the hopeful. Offer and Acceptance. 'By July we'll have 100,000 signatures of people clamouring for Munyakei to get his job back. What CBK needs to do is give him back his money. Vox Populi Vox Dei.' I was enjoying myself. A few beers under my belt. Counter offer. 'The voice of the people is the voice of God,' I grinned. He smiled. We were now co-conspirators. 'This story and the book is for you. The wazee don't work like that. Let me talk to my mzee. See what we can do. Can we meet Tuesday? Si, you want him to get his money back. We can do this thing properly. I talk to some people and you get your book out. And he gets his money. See that CBK gives him his money. 11 million is nothing. Si that's what you want?' He said this with precise chopping movements of his right hand. 'As long as we meet and he's there.' I pointed at Munyakei. The ladies were taking turns at individual photos with him. 'I also want my editor present.' 'Wee. Editor for what. Si tunaongea just me and you. You see my friend there he's the one who organised the whole evening. He took care of the budget ...' He pointed at another individual at the bar who grinned back. We shook hands and he gave me his numbers. Munyakei finished with the ladies. I overheard the ladies promising to visit him on their way to the Mara.

'Wapi huu jamaa mrefu alikuwa hapa,' he asked me. Where's that tall guy who was here?

'Jamaa mgani?' I then realized he was was talking about the Minister's son who suddenly reappeared.

'Nilikuwa naambia rafiki yako niongee na watu tuone

namna gani,' he explained to Munyakei. I was telling your friend that something can be organized once I make a few phone calls and talk to some people.

I was left with Munyakei. Later I overheard the minister's son telling his friend: 'Let's go to Cedars.' On his way out the Minister's son pointed at me. I waved, 'Enjoy Cedars,' I said. He looked at me, 'Ai Ai Ai Ai, You are not straight. All you people are not honest.' 'Wachana na yeye,' Munyakei said with nonchalance. Leave him alone. I realised that Munyakei had probably been getting under the table offers since he came back onto the public radar. Munyakei's testimony and the whole story of Goldenberg would never have emerged at the Commission if he had let himself be compromised before he appeared. He was offered several million shillings by some 'interested parties' linked to a senior politician in the current government and asked to flee to Uganda with his family. He refused and went on to testify.

Editors Note

The Goldenberg scandal cost the Kenyan Economy an approximate Ksh 68 billion - slightly more than a billion dollars at today's exchange rate - a sizeable chunk of the country's health and education budgets. Its main culprits are yet to be brought to justice.

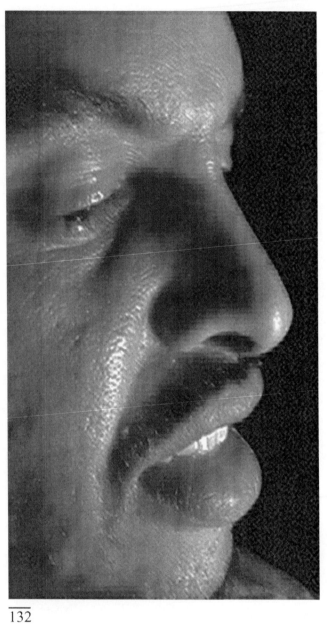

From Here To Eternity,
David Sadera Munyakei
Rest in Peace.

Billy Kahora is the editor of the Kwani? *journal. He holds a journalism degree from Rhodes University in South Africa, a post-graduate dipoma in Media Studies, and an MFA with distinction in Creative Writing from the University of Edinburgh where he was a Chevening Scholar. His writing has appeared in* Vanity Fair, *the* Mail and Guardian, *the* East African Standard, *and other publications; his story, 'Treadmill Love,' was highly commended by the 2007 Caine Prize for African Writing judges. He lives in Nairobi.*

Other **Kwani** titles

Kwani? 01 (ISBN: 9966-9836-0-0)

Kwani? 02 (ISBN: 9966-9836-2-7)

Kwani? 03 (ISBN: 9966-9836-4-3)

Kwani? 04 (ISBN: 9966-9836-6-X)

Kwani? 05, Part 1 (ISBN: 9966-7182-1-4)

Kwani? 05, Part 2 (ISBN: 9966-7182-2-2)

Kwani? Series

~Chimamanda Adichie -*Half Of a Yellow Sun* (ISBN: 9966-9836-8-6)

~Chimamanda Adichie -*Purple Hibiscus* (ISBN: 9966-9836-9-4)

~ Joseph Muthee -*Kizuizini* (ISBN: 9966-9836-7-8)

~ Ed Pavlic -*But Here Are Small Clear Refractions* (ISBN: 9966-7182-3-0)

~Billy Kahora -*The True Story of David Munyakei* (ISBN: 9966-7008-9-7)

Kwanini? Series

~Binyavanga Wainaina -*Discovering Home* (ISBN: 9966-7008-4-6)

~Binyavanga Wainaina -*Beyond River Yei* (ISBN: 9966-7008-7-0)

~Binyavanga Wainaina -*How To Write About Africa* (ISBN: 9966-7008-2-X)

~Yvonne Adhiambo Owour -*Weight of Whispers* (ISBN: 9966-7008-3-8)

~Chimamanda Adichie -*You In America* (ISBN: 9966-7008-0-3)

~Wambui Mwangi -*Internally Misplaced* (ISBN: 9966-7008-8-9)

~Richard Onyango -*The Life and Times of Richard Onyango*
(ISBN: 9966-7008-5-4)

~Mzee Ondego -*The Life of Mzee Ondego* (ISBN: 9966-7182-0-6)

~CKW -*Kwanini Special Edition* (ISBN: 9966-7008-1-1)

Lightning Source UK Ltd.
Milton Keynes UK
UKOW02f1824090115

244291UK00001B/4/P